WAY TO HAPPINESS

BOOKS BY BISHOP SHEEN:

Way to Happiness

by

MOST REVEREND FULTON J. SHEEN, PH.D., D.D.

Agrégé en Philosophie de L'Université de Louvain
Auxiliary Bishop of New York
National Director, World Mission Society for
the Propagation of the Faith

GARDEN CITY BOOKS

Garden City, New York

Plan and Purpose

THESE articles are written with a particular purpose, a special method, a deliberate spirit. The purpose will be to bring solace, healing and hope to hearts; truth and enlightenment to minds; goodness, strength and resolution to wills. The method will be the application of eternal moral and spiritual principles to the basic problems of individual and social life today. The spirit will be that of charity: love of God and love of neighbor.

And this preface will declare the basic assumptions of this book.

First: The over-emphasis on politics today is an indication that people are governed, rather than governing. The complexities of our civilization force us to organize into larger and larger units; we have become so intent on governing what is outside of us that we neglect to govern our own selves. Yet the key to social betterment is always to be found in personal betterment. Remake man and you remake his world. We gravely need to restore to man his self-respect and to give him his appropriate honor: this will keep him from bowing cravenly before those who threaten to enslave him, and it will give him the courage to defend the right, alone if need be, when the world is wrong.

Second: As society is made by man, so man, in his turn, is made by his thoughts, his decisions and his choices. Nothing ever happens to the world which did not first happen inside the mind of some man: the material of the skyscraper merely completes the architect's dream. Even the material of our physical selves is the servant of our thoughts: psychologists recognize the fact that our bodies may become tired only because of tiredness in the mind.

Worry, anxiety, fear and boredom are felt as physical: mind-fatigue appears to us as bodily fatigue.

One basic reason for tiredness of mind is the conflict in all of us between ideal and achievement, between what we ought to be and what we are, between our longing and our having, between our powers of understanding and the incomprehensible mysteries of the universe. A house divided against itself cannot stand; this perennial tension in man can be accepted and made bearable only by a surrender of the self to God. Then whatever happens is welcomed as a gift of love: frustration cannot happen to us for we have no clamorous, selfish will.

Society can be saved only if man is saved from his unbearable conflicts, and man can be rescued from them only if his soul is saved. Once, not so long ago, men put their hope of happiness in material advance; now that mood of shallow optimism has ended; the heavy burden of worry and anxiety about the future of the race and of the individual has made men conscious of their souls.

Third: Our happiness consists in fulfilling the purpose of our being. Every man knows, from his own unfulfilled hunger for them, that he was built with a capacity for three things of which he never has enough. He wants life—not for the next few minutes, but for always, and with no aging or disease to threaten it. He also wants to grasp truth—not with a forced choice between the truths of mathematics or geography, but he wants all truth. Thirdly, he wants love—not with a time-limit, not mixed with satiety or disillusionment, but love that will be an abiding ecstasy.

These three things are not to be found in this life in their completion: on earth life is shadowed by death, truth mingles with error, love is mixed with hate. But men know they would not long for these things in their purity if there were no possibility of ever finding them. So, being reasonable, they search for the source from which these mixed and imperfect portions of life, love, truth derive.

The search is like looking for the source of light in a room: it cannot come from under a chair, where light is mixed with darkness and shadow. But it can come from the sun, where light is pure with neither shadow nor darkness dulling it. In looking for the source of love, light, truth, as we know it here, we must go out beyond the limits of this shadowed world—to a Truth not mingled with its shadow, error—to a Life not mingled with its shadow, death—to a Love not mingled with its shadow, hate. We must seek for Pure Life, Pure Truth and Pure Love—and that is the definition of God. His Life is personal enough to be a Father; His Truth is personal and comprehensible enough to be a Son; His Love is so deep and spiritual that it is a Spirit.

When enough men have found this way to happiness, they will find one another in brotherhood. Social peace will then ensue.

Contents

LOVE

CHILDREN

YOUTH

MAN'S GOAL

INNER PEACE

CONTENTS

HAPPINESS

CHAPTER I

Contentment

CONTENTMENT is not an innate virtue. It is acquired through great resolution and diligence in conquering unruly desires; hence it is an art which few study. Because there are millions of discontented souls in the world today, it might be helpful for them to analyze the four main causes of discontent, and to suggest means to contentment.

The principle cause of discontent is egotism, or selfishness, which sets the self up as a primary plant around which everyone else must revolve. The second cause of discontent is envy, which makes us regard the possessions and the talents of others as if they were stolen from us. The third cause is covetousness, or an inordinate desire to have more, in order to compensate for the emptiness of our heart. The fourth cause of discontent is jealousy, which is sometimes occasioned through melancholia and sadness, and at other times by a hatred of those who have what we wish for ourselves.

One of the greatest mistakes is to think that contentment comes from something outside us rather than from a quality of the soul. There was once a boy who only wanted a marble; when he had a marble, he only wanted a ball; when he had a ball, he only wanted a top; when he had a top, he only wanted a kite, and when he had the marble, the ball, the top, and the kite, he still was not happy. Trying to make a discontented person happy is like trying to fill a sieve with water. However much you pour into it, it runs out too rapidly for you to catch up.

Nor is contentment to be found in an exchange of places. There are some who believe that if they were in a different part of the earth they would have a greater peace of soul. A goldfish, in a globe in water, and a canary in a cage, on a hot day, began talking. The fish said: "I wish I could swing like that canary; I'd like to be up there in that cage." And the canary said: "Oh, how nice to be down in that cool water where the fish is." Suddenly a voice said: "Canary, go down to the water! Fish, go up to the cage!" Immediately, they exchanged places, but neither was happy, because God originally had given each a place according to his ability, one that best suited his own nature.

The condition of our contentment is to be contained, to recognize limits. Whatever is within limits is likely to be quiet. A walled garden is one of the quietest places in the world; the world is shut out, and through its gates one can look upon it with the affection of distance, borrowing enchantment from it. So, if the soul of man is kept within limits (that is to say, not avaricious, greedy, over-reaching nor selfish), it, too, is shut into a calm, quiet, sunny contentment. Contented man, limited and bound by circumstances, makes those very limits the cure of his restlessness. It is not to the point whether a garden has one acre or three, or whether or not it has a wall; what matters is that we shall live within its bounds, whether they be large or small, in order that we can possess a quiet spirit and a happy heart.

Contentment, therefore, comes in part from faith—that is, from knowing the purpose of life and being assured that whatever the trials are, they come from the hand of a Loving Father. Secondly, in order to have contentment one must also have a good conscience. If the inner self is unhappy because of moral failures and unatoned guilt, then nothing external can give rest to the spirit. A third and final need is mortification of desires, the limitation of delights. What we over-love, we often over-grieve. Contentment enhances our enjoyment and diminishes our misery. All evils become lighter if we endure them patiently, but the greatest benefits can be poisoned by discontent. The miseries of life are sufficiently deep and extensive, without our adding to them unnecessarily.

Contentment with our worldly condition is not inconsistent with the desire for betterment. To the poorest man, Christianity says not to be merely content, but "be diligent in business." The contentment enjoined is for the time being. Man is poor today, and for this day, faith enjoins him to be satisfied; but deliverance from his poverty may be best for tomorrow, and therefore the poor man works for his increased prosperity. He may not succeed; if his poverty continues for another day, he accepts it, and then proceeds until relief comes. Thus, contentment is relative to our present state, and is not absolute in respect to the entire demands of our nature. A contented man is never poor though he have very, very little. The discontented man is never rich, let him have so very much.

CHAPTER 2

Humility

THE CHIEF CAUSE of inner unhappiness is egotism or selfishness. He who gives himself importance by boasting is actually showing the credentials of his own worthlessness. Pride is an attempt to create an impression that we are what we actually are not.

How much happier people would be if instead of exalting their ego to infinity, they reduced it to zero. They would then find the true infinite through the rarest of modern virtues: humility. Humility is truth about yourselves. A man who is six feet tall, but who says: "I am only five feet tall," is not humble. He who is a good writer is not humble if he says: "I am a scribbler." Such statements are made in order that there might be a denial and thus win praise. Rather he would be humbler who says: "Well, whatever talent I have is a gift of God and I thank Him for it." The higher the building the deeper the foundation; the greater the moral heights to which we aspire the greater the humility. As John the Baptist said when he saw Our Lord: "I must decrease; He must increase." Flowers humbly depart in the winter to see their mother roots. Dead to the world, they keep house under the earth in humble humility, unseen by the eyes of men. But because they humbled themselves, they are exalted and glorified in the new springtime.

Only when a box is empty can it be filled; only when the ego is deflated can God pour in His blessings. Some are already so stuffed with their own ego that it is impossible for love of neighbor or love of God to enter. By seeking their own constantly, everyone disowns them. But humility makes us receptive to the giving of others. You could not give unless I took. It is the taker that makes the giver. So God, before He can be Giver, must find a taker. But if one is not humble enough to receive from God, then he receives nothing.

A man possessed by the devil was brought to a Father of the Desert. When the saint commanded the devil to leave, the devil asked: "What is the difference between the sheep and the goats whom the Lord will put at His right and His left Hand the day of Judgment?" The saint answered: "I am one of the goats." The devil said: "I leave because of your humility."

Many say: "I have labored for years for others and even for God, and what did I get out of it? I am still nothing." The answer is, they have gained something; they have gained the truth of their own littleness—and of course, great merit in the next life. One day two men were in a carriage. One said: "There is not enough room for you here in this seat." The other said: "We will love each other a little more, and then there will be room enough." Ask a man: "Are you a saint?" If he answers in the affirmative, you can be very sure that he is not.

The humble man concentrates on his own errors, and not upon those of others; he sees nothing in his neighbor but what is good and virtuous. He does not carry his own faults on his back, but in front of him. The neighbor's defects he carries in a sack on his back, so he will not see them. The proud man, on the contrary, complains against everybody and believes that he has been wronged or else not treated as he deserves. When the humble man is treated badly he does not complain for he knows that he is treated better than he deserves. From a spiritual point of view, he who is proud of his intelligence, talent or voice, and never thanks God for them is a robber; he has taken gifts from God and never recognized the Giver. The ears of barley which bear the richest grain always hang the lowest. The humble man is never discouraged, but the proud man falls into despair. The humble man still has God to call upon; the proud man has only his own ego that has collapsed.

One of the loveliest prayers for humility is that of Saint Francis:

"*Lord, make me an instrument of Thy peace. Where there is hatred, let there be love; where there is injury, pardon; where there is doubt, faith; where there is despair, hope; where there is darkness, light; where there is sadness, joy. O Divine Master, grant that I may not seek so much to be consoled as to console; to be understood as to understand; to be loved as to love. For it is in giving that we receive, it is in pardon that we are pardoned, it is in dying that we are born to Eternal Life.*"

CHAPTER 3

Egotism

Egotism is a lie in action: it supposes that the egotist's whims and passions and instinctual desires take precedence over the moral law, the brotherhood of other human beings and the will of God Himself. The egotist is like a pendulum asserting its rights against the clock's, or a cloud in rebellion against the sky, or an arm insisting that it will ignore the body of which it is a part. The egotist, doing only what his own selfish desires proclaim, ends up by hating everything he does. He is like the child in the progressive school, who wailed, "Do I always *have* to do what I want?"

Self-will leads, in time, to hatred of the self. A little boy who has eaten all the ice-cream meant for the whole family comes to hate the very sight of that kind of ice-cream: and mingled with his merely animal, "conditioned" hatred of the food, is a moral loathing of himself for having committed the sin of greed. This self-hatred is the moral penalty we pay for gluttony, as the distaste for ice-cream is the physical, animal effect of the same offense.

Men who are sick with self-disgust instinctively pound their breasts, as if to drive out evil from the inner citadel of their souls. Atheists are more prone to this self-loathing than the religious man: since they do not recognize the Mercy and Love of God Who will cure us of our self-disgusts, they may carry their despair of self to the final stage of suicide. Self-destruction is a projection, an external shadowing, of the inner tragedy, in which the small self has challenged all that is greater than it and, sickened by the effects of this rebellion, has come to an unnatural hatred of its

life. Both Peter and Judas rebelled against Life when they denied
Our Lord; both of them had been warned against such a revolt;
both of them were called "devils" because of their offense; and
both repented. But Judas "repented unto himself", turned his
own ego back upon itself in the futile agony of despair. Peter,
repenting unto his Lord, emptied himself of evil through humility and regained joy.

Only submission of the self to something higher than self can
cure despair; for such humility empties the soul of both pride and
self-judgment, making room for the influx of Divine Truth and
Love. "He that humbleth himself shall be exalted; he that ex-
alteth himself shall be humbled" . . . but self-hatred is exaltation
of the self as the final, bitter judge. Until the "For Sale" sign is
hung on a soul emptied of preoccupation with the self, the Divine
Tenant cannot move in.

One test of true humility is our attitude towards praise. Anyone
who loves publicity is proud, is seeking to be justified before men;
for the humble man refers all praise to God. If he has gifts, he
knows that God gave them to him, and that they must be used to
serve their real Owner. He is like a window which is content to
let God's sunlight shine through it, with no idea that the light is
its own creation. A humble man accepts both praise and blame as
gifts from God: both the bitter and the sweet are sent by One who
loves him. As Job said, "The Lord gives, the Lord takes away;
praised be the Lord."

But the Egotist cannot forget himself, even though he suspects
and resents his own smallness: he thinks he can conceal this inferiority by always boasting of himself. The humble man is God-
surrendered, safe from despair because he knows that he is loved
by Love Itself. The egotist constantly complains that others do
not love him enough, and he fails to see that this is a result of his
own centeredness on self. His misery—like almost every other
form of unhappiness—comes from a stubborn refusal to give up
his own self-will.

Our happiest times are those in which we forget ourselves, usually in being kind to someone else. That tiny moment of self-

abdication is an act of true humility: the man who loses himself finds himself and finds his happiness.

Self-hatred and despair are diseases to which only egotists are prone. The cure for them is always the same: humility. And that means being less in love with ourselves than we are with God.

CHAPTER 4

Joy

J OY IS the delightful experience of the feelings of pleasure at a good gained and actually enjoyed or the prospect of good which one has a reasonable hope of obtaining. There can be both natural joys and spiritual joys. Natural joys would be the joy of youth before disappointment has stretched the soul, or the joy of health when food is pleasant and sweet, or the joy of success when the battle has been won, or the joys of affection when the heart is loved. All these natural joys are intensified by spiritual joys and put upon a more enduring basis. No earthly happiness would be permanent or thorough if it were not associated with a good conscience.

Spiritual joy is a serenity of temper in the midst of the changes of life, such as a mountain has when a storm breaks over it. To a man who has never rooted the soul in the Divine every trouble exaggerates itself. He cannot put his full powers to any one thing because he is troubled about many things.

A joy is not the same as levity. Levity is an act, joy a habit. Mirth is like a meteor, cheerfulness like a star; mirth is like crackling thorns, joy like a fire. Joy being more permanent makes difficult actions easier. Soldiers after a long day's march would hardly walk as nimbly as they do, if they did not march to music. A cheerful heart always finds a yoke easy and a burden light.

Certainly no nurse is helpful in a sick room unless she has the spirit of cheerfulness. Every nurse really ought to have two things before she enters a sick room: an incision and a sense of humor. An incision in order that she may know the value of pain; a sense of humor in order that she may know how to diffuse happiness.

This incision need not be physical but it should at least be symbolic, in the sense that there should be a deep appreciation of the woes and sufferings of others. There is nothing that so much adds to the longevity of sickness as a long face.

Joy has much more to do with the affections than with reason. To the man with a family his wife and children call out and sustain his delights much more than his intellect could ever stimulate. Standing before a cradle a father seems face to face with the attributes of the everlasting Being Who has infused His tenderness and love into the babe. The power of rejoicing is always a fair test of a man's moral condition. No man can be happy on the outside who is already unhappy on the inside. If a sense of guilt weighs down the soul no amount of pleasure on the outside can compensate for the loss of joy on the inside. As sorrow is attendant on sin, so joy is the companion of holiness.

Joy can be felt in both prosperity and adversity. In prosperity it consists not in the goods we enjoy but in those we hope for; not in the pleasures we experience but in the promise of those which we believe without our seeing. Riches may abound but those for which we hope are the kind which moths do not eat, rust consume, nor thieves break through and steal. Even in adversity there can be joy in the assurance that the Divine Master Himself died through the Cross as the condition of His Resurrection.

If joy be uncommon today it is because there are timid souls who have not the courage to forget themselves and to make sacrifices for their neighbor, or else because the narrower sympathies make the brighter things of the world to come, appear as vanities. As the pull from the belief in God and the salvation of the soul fade from life, so also joy vanishes and one returns to the despair of the heathens. The old Greeks and Romans always saw a shadow across their path and a skeleton at their feet. It was no surprise that one day a Roman who had nothing to live for, nothing to hope for, entered his bath and opened a vein and so bled quietly and painlessly to death. A famous Greek poet once said of life that it was better not to be born, and the next best thing was to quit life as soon as possible. All this is at the other extreme from St. Paul, who said: "Rejoice in the Lord always and again I say, Rejoice."

CHAPTER 5

Is Modern Man Far from Peace?

No one is dangerously unhappy except the individual who does not know what happiness means. Life is unbearable only to those who are ignorant of why they are alive; men in such a condition of soul equate happiness with pleasure (which is a very different matter) and identify joy with a tingling of the nerve-endings (which it is not). But things which are external to us never bring us inner peace. The more persistently anyone looks for satisfaction and a goal to serve in something outside of his control, the less stable he will find it, the more subject he will be to disappointments.

There are two movements towards happiness. The first of these is our withdrawal from the outside . . . from too great an absorption in the things of the world. The second movement is far more profound: it is an ascension from what is inferior within us to what is its superior, from our egotism to our God. Modern man has experienced the first movement; exterior things have become so many sources of misery to him. Wars, depressions, the insecurity and emptiness of life have so terrified men that they have tried to close off their contacts with the outside world and have begun to seek for satisfactions in their own limited selves. That is why psychiatry is having such a field-day: the modern soul, alarmed at what it finds without, has drawn down the shades and begun to look for contentment in analyzing its own unconsciousness, anxieties and fears, its doldrums and frustrations.

But such self-containment can prove a prison if one is locked into it with his own ego alone, for there is no more confining strait-jacket in the world than that of the self left *to* itself. The cure never lies in using a psychoanalytic scalpel to release the inner moral pus and watch it flow; that is a morbid act for both the patient and the doctor. The cure, rather, consists in discovering why one is lonely, and afraid of solitude—for most people have a dread of being alone, without knowing why the prospect frightens them.

The problem of our day is this problem of finding interior peace, and it is in this that the twentieth century is marked off from the nineteenth. A hundred years ago men looked to the exterior world for the answers to their problems: they worshipped science or nature, expected happiness to come from progress or politics or profits. The twentieth century man is worried about himself: he is even more concerned over the problem of sex than by sex itself —is interested in the mental attitude he should take towards it, rather than in its physical satisfaction and the begetting of children. His own values, moods and attitudes absorb him.

Although a great deal of nonsense has been written about the interior life of men in our day, it is still true that the twentieth century is closer to God than the nineteenth century was. We are living on the eve of one of the great spiritual revivals of human history. Souls are sometimes closest to God when they feel themselves farthest away from Him, at the point of despair. For an empty soul, the Divine can fill; a worried soul, the Infinite can pacify. A self-concerned, proud soul, however, is inaccessible to Grace.

Modern man has been humiliated: neither his proud expectations of progress nor of science have turned out as he hoped. Yet he has not quite reached the point of humbling himself. He is still imprisoned in the self, and able to see nothing else beyond. The psychoanalysts may be allowed to bore into his thoughts for a few years more; but the time is not far off when modern men will utter a frantic appeal to God to lift them from the empty cistern of their own egos. St. Augustine knew it well: he said, "Our hearts are restless until they rest in Thee."

That is why—although a catastrophic war may threaten us— the times are not as bad as they seem. Modern man has not yet returned to God; but he has, at least, returned to himself. Later he will surpass and transcend himself with God's grace, which he is seeking, even now. No one ever looked for something unless he knew that it existed; today the frustrated soul is looking for God, as for the memory of a name he used to know.

The difference between those who have found God in faith and those who are still seeking Him is like the difference between a wife, happy in the enjoyment of her husband's companionship, and a young girl wondering if she will ever find a husband, and perhaps trying to attract men by the wrong approach. Those who search for pleasure, fame and wealth are all seeking the Infinite, but the seekers are still on the outskirts of the Eternal City. Those with faith have penetrated to their real home within the Infinite and have found the "peace which the world cannot give." As one can see a figure far off and not yet recognize him as a long-lost friend, so one can sense the need of the Infinite and desire the endless ecstasy of love, but not yet know that it is God.

It makes no difference how wicked a soul may be, there is no one subjecting himself to illicit pleasures who does not have a consciousness of his subjection and his slavery. Perhaps that is why alcoholics are often liars; their lips deny a slavery which their lives so visibly witness. Such individuals, unwilling to admit themselves mistaken, still refuse to be convinced of Divine Truth; but their sadness and their emptiness will eventually drive them to the God of Mercy.

Our exterior world today is in desperate straits, but the inner world of man is far from hopeless. The world of politics and economics lags behind the psychological development of men themselves. The world is far from God, but human hearts are not. That is why peace will come less from political changes than from man himself, who, driven to take refuge within his own soul from the turmoil without, will be lifted above himself to the happiness for which he was made.

CHAPTER 6

The Ego and the Moral Law

THE GREAT PSYCHOLOGISTS of the ages have universally agreed that the root of all unhappiness is selfishness or egotism. Egotism is the rejection of the double command to love God and neighbor, and the affirmation of the self as the standard of all truth and morality.

Those who live enclosed in their own ego pass through three mental stages, the first of which is *self-indulgence*. Once the ego is made absolute, then every other person, event, and thing becomes a *means* to the gratification of the self. In youth, the ego desires satisfaction of its own flesh, without regard to personalities; in middle age, it craves power; and in old age, it often sublimates into avarice and love of "security." Those who deny the immortality of the soul, almost always substitute for it the immortality of the means of subsistence. The severance of pleasure from God always ends in the abandonment to the sensate.

Since self-indulgence at all times is impossible, not only because it comes in conflict with other self-indulgent individuals, but also because the pleasure diminishes with use, the ego finally descends to the second mental stage of *fear*. Fear is fossilized self-love. He whose life has been most exteriorized, by seeking pleasures wholly outside self, is most subject to the dread of loss, because he has put his trust in those things which are least subject to the control of his will. The more a man leans on a stick that belongs to another egotist, the more liable he is to its removal and a fall! Disappointment is the lot of those who live wholly on the level of the senses! Every pessimist is a frustrated hedonist!

Disappointments, satiety, and fed-up-ness produce fear. The greater the egotism, the greater the fear; the more selfish the individual, the blacker his dreads. The whole environment becomes black with foes: "Everybody is against me." Some fear old age, others death, others suicide, until finally despair settles in, which is the ego left to its resources, which it finally admits are nothing.

The third stage is *ignorance*. Because egotism cuts off communion with God and with neighbor, it thereby cuts off knowledge from both these sources. It has left only the knowledge of its own distress. The ego becomes increasingly unaware of its destiny and purpose in life. It may gather facts, but it can not put them together. Its knowledge becomes like courses in a modern college, which are collected to get a credit, but not to give a philosophy of life. Ignorance multiplies as a man knows many things which cannot be correlated. The wise man knows *one thing*, which is Goodness, and all else is unified in it. But the ignorance of the egotist embitters and makes him cynical; first, because he can never loose himself from the desire of Goodness, which God implanted in his soul; and secondly, because he knows that he no longer has the power to will it.

These tragic effects of self-love are not without a remedy. Christianity, curiously enough, begins with the assumption that many humans are selfish. The Divine Command to love God and neighbor as thyself has behind it the assumption that every man does love himself. Those two little words, *as thyself,* break all self-love. They bring up the question how does a man love himself. There is always something a man likes about himself and something he does not like about himself. He likes his life, so he sits in an easy chair, wears the clothes which fit, nourishes his body, etc. But there is something he does not like about himself. He does not like himself when he makes a fool of himself, or when he insults a friend. In other words, he likes himself as a creature made to the image and likeness of God. He does not like himself when he spoils that image. So the neighbor is to be loved. He is to be loved as a person; and even as a sinner, for a sinner is a person. But his sin is not to be loved, because that is the blurring of the

Divine resemblance. More concretely, one is to love the Communists and hate Communism.

There is only one escape from this law, and that is to quarrel as to who is the neighbor, as the lawyer did. Our Lord answered that the neighbor is not necessarily the man who lives next door. He is the one whom we regard as an enemy. But the Lord did not exclude the possibility that the enemy may also live next door!

CHAPTER 7

Detachment

Life seems flat and stale to many people: they wonder why they do not grow or stretch, improve or learn. They believe themselves to be in a rut. They would like to know how to get out of it.

The answer to this problem is simple, although applying it is never easy. It is *detachment* which such men and women need.

Detachment is a matter of cutting all the strands that tie us to the ground. Thus allowing the soul to bound upwards toward God. We are like balloons; we can be held down by steel cables or by threads as thin as gossamer, but until they are cut, we are never free from attachment to the everyday things which hold us down, make us their slaves.

Souls can be pledged to any number of trivial, cramping things in the outside world. They may come to depend on a constant succession of pleasures, on excitement, on hourly news dispatches, on cocktail parties, so that the inner life has hardly time to exist. Whenever we become dependent on an external thing, so that we cannot find happiness without it, our inner life is reduced: all the "extras" which the body *has* to have are charged up to the soul. The phrase, "I can take it or leave it alone," is a good one to apply to many things besides drink: it should be our attitude toward every external prop to happiness.

If we "need" outside things, we become literally absorbed in them, so that our own personalities are dispersed. We are like a well which has been pumped so constantly that all its waters are absorbed by the alien clay. Some people are so given over to the external that, robbed of some pleasures or possessions, they feel they hardly exist at all. They have learned to esteem their own value in terms of having, rather than of being. Such souls may, if deprived of their savings and wealth, commit suicide: their fealty to things is so great that they have lost all knowledge of their true relationship to God.

The remedy for such a dangerous and unhappy state of attachment is a gradual loosening of the ties that bind us to external things. We must cease to be other-possessed . . . by alcohol, or noise, by success or pleasure. In such a simple matter as reaching for a cigaret, it is wise for us to let the human will decide, for or against, instead of responding to the stimulus whenever it occurs. Even lawful and harmless pleasures should be refused, from time to time, so that we do not belong to them, or to our selfish whims. For the man who lives only for his own impulses keeps very bad company.

Certain natives of Australia do not know how to count above three. They say, "One. Two. Three. Enough." Their philosophy of economics puts a limit on externals, and probably makes them more carefree than we, who count by billions.

Men live by their desires, but it is possible for us to choose whether we will desire things of the spirit or of the world. The man or woman who can look back on his day and count five times when he has refused to yield to some minute whim is on the way to inner growth: he has held himself back and rejected the slavery of things.

Attachment is narrowing; detachment broadens us. The materialist has a confined personality because he lives in a closed universe, no larger than the things he can reach with his senses. The egotist lives in an even narrower world: the padded cell of his own selfishness. The believer has broken free—he can ascend freely to the Heaven on earth in which his nature can expand towards a limitless and self-forgetful joy.

CHAPTER 8

Return to Nothingness

GOD MADE US out of nothing . . . nothing at all . . . and it is well for us occasionally to recall that fact. Because God made us, we are precious; but because we came from utter nothingness, we can never boast of our self-sufficiency. And since we came from God, we have an insatiable craving to revert to union with His Life and Truth and Love. But since we are also the children of nothingness, we are as dependent on Him as the sun-rays on the sun.

When John the Baptist saw Our Lord for the first time, this sense of nothingness caused him to say, "I must decrease; He must increase." This did not involve St. John in any false humility, any unrealistic pretence that he or his work was worthless. It was a simple admission that even the brilliant star must lose its luster in the rising glory of the sun.

John diminished himself in the face of God; we might do the same, reminding ourselves, from time to time, that nothingness is our origin. We can do this by the practice of humility . . . . . and out of such an act our creation is renewed. We can return psychologically to the womb of nothingness, our mother, by emptying ourselves of all that is not God, and so returning to that naked naught from which He drew us forth.

When we look the true facts of our existence in the face, we must see that He is all, and that we possess nothing which did not come from Him. We realize, then, that He holds us in existence, from moment to moment. We become aware of the fact that without Him, we can do nothing. Our Divine Saviour reminded his followers of their relative nothingness when he described the

proper behavior for Christians at a banquet: they should not bolt
to the head-table, setting themselves up as VIP's; they should act
as nobodies, rather than trying to appear as somebodies. A little
later in His ministry, He reverted to the theme and praised the
publican who sought the back of the temple in admission of his
nothingness, instead of the Pharisee who pushed himself forward.
Our Lord gave Heaven's verdict: "Everyone who exalts himself
will be humbled, and the man who humbles himself will be exalted."

The injunction to be humble does not, however, mean that we
should go through life with an "inferiority complex." We are not
to seek the valley of humiliation in order to cower there in darkness—but rather so that, from that valley, we may see the mountains of God and find our exaltation there. The upswing from a
sense of the littleness of the self to joy in the greatness of the Lord
is beautifully expressed in the words of Mary, the Mother of
Jesus: "He has looked graciously upon the lowliness of His hand-
maid." Mary's recognition of her own "nothingness" apart from
God had carried her lower in her own esteem than anyone who
ever lived; thus her exaltation was correspondingly more sublime.

The more we think of ourselves, the less we think of God; all
egotists are anti-religious. The spiritual prerequisite for seeing
God is not to be blinded by our own ego with its pride, conceit
and deification of the self. Only the empty can be filled; only
the de-egotized can be divinized. The well-water cannot add to
the cup already filled to the brim with mud; and only the humble,
emptied soul can be filled by the Waters of Everlasting Life. Often
during our lifetimes we fill our cups with the mud and stones of
selfishness. This mud, this false pride, this exaggeration of the
worth of the self apart from God is what complicates life and
prevents the soul from being united with That for which it was
made. As the haze prevents the sun's rays from shining on the
earth, so the self, denying the nothingness which is its reality, cuts
off God. And as the sun in time dissolves the haze by its heat, so
God, too, may burn away our pride and reach the soul.

God Himself showed us the way of humility; He descended
into nothingness when He humbled Himself to the lowly death of

the Crucifixion, only to rise in His glory, drawn up by the irresistible force of Divine Power. For us, too, the only avenue to God is through a Crucifixion of the self. The self-made man builds on his own ego . . . . . and generally reveals himself as a poor architect. But the God-made man—too contemptuous of self to use it as a rafter or a corner-stone—lets God erect the edifice of his life. He is like St. Paul: "I am what I am by the grace of God," and he is happy in his frank humility.

CHAPTER 9

The Subterranean

THE MODERN WORLD has a strange love of the subterranean . . . of the deep, dark cellars of human living, of plunging into and analyzing the sub-human areas of our lives. This attraction is, in part, a reaction from the opposite extreme. A century ago men believed themselves to have reached a new and higher plateau of living. They spoke of inevitable progress, of conquering death, of making men into gods, of turning the earth into a Paradise.

Now, the presumption of our grandfathers has yielded to the despair of men in our own times. Man, who got vertigo on his unnatural heights, has fallen into a most terrible despair in the depths. His over-enthusiasm has yielded to disgust, his hope for greater pleasure to satiety, his over-indulgence in heady hopes of temporal success have given way to nausea.

Two groups of experts in the subterranean have come along in modern times: one of them analyzes the workers, under the aspect of the "masses", the other studies the unconscious mind of the individual man. People become "masses", who can be manipulated by a dictator, only when they have lost their sense of responsibility and self-control. In such a state they may become the prey of alien, external forces; that marks the first requirement of the totalitarian state. The Communists and Fascists study this.

The second group of experts in the subterranean are the men who take as their field the sub-rational, involuntary, sub-human part of man's intelligence: his subconscious mind, into which the mind throws its rejected scraps of thought. The subconscious mind has, in fact, an influence on human conduct; but it is not the only factor, nor the finally determining one. A flaw in the acorn from which it sprung may explain some of the shape of the grown oak-tree; but light and heat and the invisible forces of life are also responsible for its present state.

These twin groups of students of the subterranean give us a clue to our age; for men have always tended to think of hell as being in the nether regions, as Virgil did: and although the Church has never discoursed on the geography of hell, the popular imagination places it under ground. As a result, whenever the public interest veers towards the "sub-" anything, there is a psychological possibility that the question of hell may be in the back of the minds of a whole generation of thinkers and readers.

Those who rivet their attention on the unconscious . . . those who hope that by study of the libido and the sex-instincts they may solve the problems of their lives . . . are seeking happiness in the "sub-" regions, where it is never found. It is only from use of the reason and the will (which are God-like) that human beings may find peace. The tragedy of our day is the despair of the successful: their misery does not originate in the failure of their plans, but in the fact that, having realized them, they found no happiness. The Everything they longed to have (material benefits and temporal triumphs) turned out, on possession, to be Nothing. And Nothing is the polar opposite to God and His creation. Hell is the ego, sated with its own satisfied wishes, having to consume itself forever with no hope of release.

The world today awaits a resurrection. The masses who are submerged by dictatorial powers await the breaking of the serpent's neck, so that they may become free to act on their own authority, as they did when our Constitution was written. For it stated that, "We the *people* of the United States", ordained and established a government. In a similar way, individual souls who are locked in the misery of the unconscious selves . . . who are operating on a sub-human level of animal and instinctive behavior . . . need a resurrection to carry them up from the grave in which their satiety has placed them. They, too, are longing for the light.

There is a life in the egg, but for the life to emerge, the shell must be broken. There is also life in the despoiled masses, and in the buried, frustrated individual souls. But for both of them, too, the shell containing them has to be broken, and broken from without. It will take a Power which is not human, but Divine, to break it.

What every soul must ask itself is: Do I want to go on living in that shell, or am I willing to be brought to a point of spiritual incubation? Those inside the shells can get out if they will allow God to free them by smashing the egotistical shell in which they hover away from His light.

It is a serious question to answer. And those who refuse to take seriously any moral or spiritual question end by taking Nothingness seriously, which is the area of the eternal subterranean. But if we take the soul seriously, then we are able to take everything else rather lightly. This is the beginning of happiness, here and hereafter.

CHAPTER 10

The Need of Revolution

NIETZSCHE, the nineteenth century philosopher, tried to express the temper of his age in the statement, "God is dead"— by which he meant that men, in his period, were losing their faith. He also cast a prophetic eye towards the future and foretold that the twentieth century would be one of wars and revolutions. His two statements were associated by a deeper logic than the inventor of the "superman" philosophy knew: men who have ceased to love God will not love their neighbors for very long— and they will find particular difficulty in trying to love that special neighbor, their enemy.

This is, indeed, a century of revolutions. But it need not go down in history as a period when revolutions were entirely economic and political. There is always the possibility open to us of making ours the time of glorious revolutions, of revolutions against ourselves. A revolution is involved whenever any soul dethrones the ego which has mastered him and submits, instead, to the principle of love. A revolution occurs whenever humility replaces pride in us, and we abandon the foolish striving for "success" and notoriety.

This type of home-made revolution has its pattern in the action of Our Lord Himself; the night before He died for the redemption of the world, He knelt before His followers, as if He were least of them all. Earlier in His teaching life, He had often told them not to seek the first seats at the table, not to desire to be known among men. When the Apostles disputed among themselves as to which of them was greatest, He called for a revolution in their values.

He had told them: "The kings of the Gentiles lord it over them, and those who rule over them win the name of benefactors. With you, it is not to be so; no difference is to be made among you between the greatest and the youngest of all, between him who commands and him who serves. Tell me, which is greater: the man who sits at table, or the man who serves him? Surely, the man who sits at table; yet I am here among you, as your servant."

Our Lord had instituted the revolution of humility in words before; now He put it into practice after the Last Supper, when "He laid his garments aside, took a towel and put it about him; and then he poured water into the basin, and began to wash the feet of his disciples, wiping them with the towel that girded him." Slaves were assigned, in those days, to such menial tasks as this. It was a topsy-turvy event on a gigantic scale to have the Master of Masters, the King of Kings kneel down at twenty-four calloused, sweaty feet and make them clean—as His absolution still makes clean our calloused hearts and our soiled souls. All human values were forever reversed in the startling revolution Christ declared in the words: "The man who exalts himself will be humbled, and the man who humbles himself will be exalted."

At the moment these words were uttered, Caesar lost his throne. The principle of exploitation was undone, and arrogance and pride were shown the door. From now on, all Christians had been warned against judging as the world judges, against seeking for themselves the rewards the world can give. As water dropped from His hands that night, the old systems of morality were rendered obsolete, and the noblest concepts of the ancients became inadequate for man. From now on, the worst of all possible disorders of the soul were known: they were the failure to serve others, the accounting of oneself as being worthy of a special privilege. A new law had been born: it revealed the equality of all men before God, and went on to declare the beauty of humility. He Who had humbled Himself by becoming man now multiplied the gift and underscored the lesson when He reduced His infinity to the service of His servants.

Revolution within the soul is the Christian adventure. It requires no hatred, demands no personal rights, claims no exalted titles, tells no lies. In such a revolution, it is love which bores from within and acts as a Fifth Column, loyal to God, within our tangled and disordered selves. Such a revolution destroys the pride and selfishness, the envy and jealousy and longing to be "first" which makes us intolerant of others' rights. The sword it carries is not turned against our neighbor, but against our absurd over-valuation of the self. In other revolutions, it is easy to fight, for it is against the "evil enemy" that we are at war. But the Christian revolution is difficult, for the enemy we must assault is a part of us. Yet this is the only revolution that ever issues in true peace: other rebellions are never ended, for they stop short of their goal: they leave hatred still simmering in the soul of man.

Contemporary thinking is directed towards a revolution in the external world of nations and classes, races and parties and cliques. But Our Divine Lord did not take as His first task the social revolution; He first remade individual man through the Resurrection and then, later, by sending His spirit into man, He regenerated the old world's society.

St. Augustine said: "They that perturb the peace they live in, do it not for hate of it, but to show their power in the alteration of it." Wars come when men project their inner conflicts onto the outside world; peace will come when many men have waged the inner revolution in which their pride is broken and their selfish ambition is destroyed. The peace that follows on such spiritual warfare can act as a happy contagion from soul to soul, bringing peace on earth to all men of good will.

CHAPTER II

Joy from the Inside

EACH OF US makes his own weather, determines the color of the skies in the emotional universe which he inhabits. We can, by a creative effort, bring such sunlight to our souls that it makes radiant whatever events may come our way. We can, on the other hand, permit ourselves to slump into a state of inner depression so deep and filled with gloom that only the most intense outward stimulations of the senses are able to rouse us from our apathy.

Everyone must have pleasure, the philosophers tell us. The man who has integrated his personality in accordance with its nature, and oriented his life towards God knows the intense and indestructible pleasure the saints called joy. No outward event can threaten him or ruffle his happiness. But many men look outward for their pleasure and expect the accidents of their lives to provide their happiness. Since nobody can make the universe his slave, everyone who looks outward for pleasure is bound to disappointment. A glut of entertainment wearies us; a realized ambition becomes a bore; a love that promised full contentment loses its glamour and its thrill. Lasting happiness can never come from the world. Joy is not derived from the things we get or the people we meet; it is manufactured by the soul itself, as it goes about its self-forgetful business.

The secret of a happy life is the moderation of our pleasures in exchange for an increase of joy. But several contemporary practices make this difficult for us. One of these is the type of merchandising which tries to increase our desires in order that we shall buy more goods. Allied with this, is the spoiled-child psychology of modern man, which tells him that he is entitled to get anything he wants, that the world owes everyone the satisfaction of his whims. Once the ego has become the center around which everything else revolves, we are vulnerable: our peace can be destroyed by a draft from an open window, by our inability to buy a coat made of some exotic fur so rare that only twenty women in the world can wear it—by our failure to get invited to a luncheon, or our failure to pay the biggest income-tax in the nation. The ego is always insatiable, if it is in command; no indulgences and no honors quiet its craving, either for "madder music and for a stronger wine," or for the heady delights of testimonial dinners and 72-point headlines.

The ego-centered men view as calamities the denial of any of their wishes: they want to dominate their world, to pull its puppet-strings and force those about them to obey their will. If such an ego's wishes are crossed and checked by another ego, its owner is in despair. Occasions for despondency and sadness are thus multiplied, for all of us are bound to be denied some of the things we want—it is our choice whether this loss shall be accepted with a cheerful good grace or taken as an outrage and an affront to us.

Today millions of men and women consider that their happiness is destroyed if they must get along without a few things of which their grandfathers had never dreamed. Luxuries have become necessities to them; and the more things a man needs in order to be happy, the more he has increased his chances of disappointment and despair. Whim has become his master, trivia his tyrant; he no longer is self-possessed, but he has become possessed by outward objects, trumpery toys.

Plato in his "Republic" wrote of the man whose life is run by his whims and fancies; his words were written 2,300 years ago, but they are still pat today: "Often he will take to politics, leaping to his feet, and do or say whatever comes into his head; or he conceives an admiration for a general and his interests turn to war; or for a man of business, and straightway that is his line. He knows no order or necessity in life; he will not listen to anyone who tells him that some pleasures come in the gratification of good and noble desires, others from evil ones, and that the former should be fostered and encouraged, the latter disciplined and chained. To all such talk, he shakes his head and says that all enthusiasms are similar and worthy of equal attention."

Pleasures must be arranged in a hierarchy if we are to get the greatest enjoyment out of life. The most intense and lasting joys come only to those who are willing to practice a certain self-restraint, to undergo the boredom of a preliminary discipline. The best view is from the mountain-top, but it may be arduous to reach it. No man ever enjoyed reading Horace without drilling himself with the declensions of his grammar first. Full happiness is understood only by those who have denied themselves some legitimate pleasures in order to obtain deferred joys. Men who "let themselves go," go to seed or go mad. The Saviour of the world Himself told us that the best joys come only after we have purchased them by prayer and fasting: we must give up our copper pennies first, out of love for Him, and He will pay us back in pieces of gold, in joy and ecstasy.

CHAPTER 12

Love Is Infinite

THERE is a profound difference in quality between the possessions that we need, and use, and actually enjoy, and the accumulation of useless things we accumulate out of vanity or greed or the desire to surpass others. The first kind of possession is a legitimate extension of our personalities: we enrich a much-used object by our love, and it becomes dear to us. We can learn about the two kinds of ownership in any nursery: a child who has only a single toy enriches it with his love. The spoiled child, with many play-things spread out for him, quickly becomes blasé and ceases to take pleasure in any one of them. The quality of his love diminishes with the number of objects offered for his love . . . as a river has less depth, the more it spreads over the plains.

When we visit a large mansion, inhabited by only two people, we feel the coldness of such a house, too vast to be made a home by human love. Each of us, by his presence, can ennoble a few cubic feet . . . but no more. The more people own beyond the limit of things they can personalize and love, the more they will suffer boredom, ennui and satiety.

Yet men and women are forever trying to add to their possessions far beyond the limit of enjoyment. This is because of their mistaken belief that their hunger for Infinity can be satisfied by an infinity of material things: what they really wish is the Infinity of Divine Love.

Our imaginations are easily misled into desiring a false infinity, when once we begin to long for "wealth". For "wealth" and "money" are things that appeal to the imagination, which is insatiable in its wishes. Real goods, such as those our bodies need, have not this quality: there is a narrow limit to the amount of food our stomachs will hold and when that is reached, we do not wish for more. Our Lord fed the five thousand in the desert with fish and bread, and all of them had their fill. But if He had given them, instead, $20,000 war bonds, no single person would have said, "One is enough for me."

Credit-wealth . . . stocks, bonds, bank-balances . . . have no set limit, at which we say, "No more". They have in them a caricature-infinity, which allows men to use them as false religions, as substitutes for the true Infinity of God. Like money, love and power can become *ersatz* religions: those who pursue these things as ends will never find satisfaction. Such men are all in pursuit of God, but they do not know His name, nor where to look for Him.

Since every increase in quantity among the things we love brings a decrease in the quality of love, there are two ways by which we may hope to keep love pure. One is to give away in proportion as we receive: this habit reminds us that we are merely trustees of God's riches, not their rightful owners. Yet few people risk doing this: they are afraid to touch their "capital", and every cent they add to it becomes part of the sacred pile which must not be disturbed. They become identified with what they love; if it is wealth, they cannot bear to part with any portion of its accumulated burden.

The second way of preserving ourselves from an unseemly greed is the heroic way . . . the way of complete detachment from wealth, as practiced by St. Francis of Assisi and all those who take the vows of poverty. There is a paradox in such a renunciation, for the man who has given up even the hope of "security" is the richest man in the world; he is the most secure of all of us, for he wants nothing . . . and that is a boast that no millionaire can make. Everyone's power of renunciation is greater than anyone's power to possess: no man can own the earth, but any man can disown it.

The misers may fill their wallets, but never their hearts, for they cannot obtain all the wealth they are able to imagine and desire. But the poor in heart are rich in happiness. God gave us love enough to spend in getting back to Him so that we could find Infinity there; he did not give us love enough to hoard.

CHAPTER 13

The Philosophy of Pleasure

We all want happiness. We should all take the sensible step of learning that there are three laws of pleasure which, if followed, will make the attainment of happiness immeasurably easier.

The first law: If you are ever to have a good time, you cannot plan your life to include nothing but good times. Pleasure is like beauty; it is conditioned by contrast. A woman who wants to show off her black velvet dress will not, if she is wise, stand against a black curtain, but against a white curtain. She wants the contrast. Fireworks would not delight us if they were shot off against a background of fire, or in the blaze of the noonday sun: they need to stand out against the darkness. Lilies bring us a special pleasure because their petals rise, surprisingly, on the waters of foul ponds. Contrast is needed to help us see each thing as being vividly itself.

Pleasure, by the same principle, is best enjoyed when it comes to us as a "treat," in contrast to experiences that are less pleasurable. We make a great mistake if we try to have all our nights party-night. No one would enjoy Thanksgiving if every dinner were a turkey dinner. New Year's Eve would not delight us if the whistles blew at midnight every night.

Fun rests on contrast, and so does the enjoyment of a funny situation. If a Bishop has a mitre thrust on the side of his head by an errant master of ceremonies, it makes us laugh; it would not be funny if all Bishops always wore their mitres askew.

Our enjoyment of life is vastly increased if we follow the

spiritual injunction to bring some mortification and self-denial into our lives. This practice saves us from being jaded; it preserves the tang and joy of living. The harp-strings of our lives are not thin, made slack by being pulled until they are out of tune; instead, we tighten them and help preserve their harmony.

Self-discipline brings back to us the excitement of our childhood, when our pleasures were rationed—when we got our dessert at the end of the meal and never at the start.

The second law: Pleasure is deepened and enhanced when it has survived a moment of tedium or pain: this law helps us to make our prized pleasures last for a whole lifetime. To do so, we must keep going at anything we do until we get our second wind. One enjoys a mountain-climb more after passing through the first moment of discouraged exhaustion. One becomes more interested in a job of work after the first impulse to drop it has been overcome.

In the same way, marriages become stable only after disillusionment has brought the honeymoon to an end. The great value of the marital vow is in keeping the couple together during the first quarrel; it tides them over their early period of resentment, until they get the second wind of true happiness at being together. Married joys, like all great joys, are born out of some pain. As we must crack the nut to taste the sweet so, in the spiritual life, the cross must be the prelude to the crown.

The third law: Pleasure is a by-product, not a goal. Happiness must be our bridesmaid, not our bride. Many people make the great mistake of aiming directly at pleasure; they forget that pleasure comes only from the fulfillment of a duty or obedience to a law—for man is made to obey the laws of his own nature as inescapably as he must obey the law of gravity. A boy has pleasure eating ice-cream because he is fulfilling one of the "oughts" of human nature: eating. If he eats more ice-cream than the laws of his body sanction, he will no longer get the pleasure he seeks, but the pain of a stomach ache. To seek pleasure, regardless of law, is to miss it.

Shall we start with pleasure or end with it? There are two

answers to the question: the Christian and the pagan. The Christian says, "Begin with the fast and end with the feast, and you will really savor it." The pagan says, "Begin with the feast and end with the morning-after headache."

WORK

CHAPTER 14

Work

Very few people in this age do the kind of work they like to do. Instead of choosing their jobs from choice, they are forced by economic necessity to work at tasks which fail to satisfy them. Many of them say, "I ought to be doing something bigger," or "This job of mine is only important because I get paid." Such an attitude lies at the bottom of much unfinished and badly-executed work. The man who chooses his work because it fulfills a purpose he approves is the only one who grows in stature by working. He alone can properly say, at the end of it, "It is finished!"

This sense of vocation is sadly lacking nowadays. The blame should not be placed on the complexity of our economic system, but on a collapse of our spiritual values. Any work, viewed in its proper perspective, can be used to ennoble us; but a necessary prelude to seeing this is to understand the philosophy of labor.

Every task we undertake has two aspects—our purpose, which makes us think it worth doing, and the work itself, regarded apart from its end-purpose. We play tennis to get exercise; but we play the game as well as possible, just for the joy of doing the thing well. The man who argued that he could get as much exercise by sloppy technique on the courts would have missed an understanding of the second aspect of all activity: the accomplishment of the task in accordance with its own standards of excellence. In the same way, a man working in an automobile factory may have, as his primary purpose, the earning of wages; but the purpose of the work itself is the excellent completion of the task.

A workman should be aware of the second purpose at all times—as the artist is aware of the aim of beauty in his painting and the housewife is aware of the need for neatness when she dusts.

Today the first aspect of working has become paramount, and we tend to ignore the second . . . so that many workmen lead half-lives in their laboring hours. They are like gardeners, ordered to grow cabbage to give them sauerkraut juice, but indifferent as to whether their plots are weeded properly or their cabbages are healthy vegetables. This is a mistaken attitude: God Himself worked when He made the world and then, viewing it, He called it "good."

The legitimate pride in doing work well relieves it of much of its drudgery. Some people, who have held to this craftsman's standard, get a thrill from any job they do. They know the satisfaction of "a job well done" whether they are engaged in caning a chair or cleaning a horse's stall or carving a statue for a Cathedral. Their honor and their self-respect are heightened by the discipline of careful work. They have retained the old attitude of the middle ages, when work was a sacred event, a ceremony, a source of spiritual merit. Labor was not then undertaken merely for the sake of economic gain, but was chosen through an inner compulsion, through a desire to project the creative power of God through our own human effort.

No task should be undertaken in a spirit which ignores either of these two primary aspects of work. To link together the two things . . . the joy of making a table well with the purpose of making it at all, which is to earn a living . . . the following principles should be kept in mind:

(1) Work is a moral duty and not, as many men imagine, a mere physical necessity. St. Paul said, *"The man who refuses to work must be left to starve."* When work is seen as a moral duty, it is apparent that it not only contributes to the social good, but also performs further services to the worker himself: it prevents the idleness from which many evils can arise and it also keeps his body in subjection to the reasoned will.

(2) *"To work is to pray."* The well-regulated life does not defer prayer until work has been accomplished; it turns the work it-

self into a prayer. We accomplish this when we turn to God at the beginning and completion of each task and mentally offer it up for love of Him. Then, whether we are nursing a child or making carburetors, turning a lathe or running an elevator, the task is sanctified. No amount of piety in leisure hours can compensate for slipshod labor on the job. But any honest task, well done, can be turned into a prayer.

(3) A medieval economist, Antonio of Florence, summed up the relationship of work to life in the happy formula: *"The object of making money is that we may provide for ourselves and our dependents. The object of providing for self and others is that one may live virtuously. The object of living virtuously is to save our souls and attain eternal happiness."*

Work should, in justice, receive two kinds of reward—for it is not only individual, but also social. John Jones, who works in a mine, is tired at the end of the day: this is his individual sacrifice. For it he receives his wages. But John Jones has also, during the day, made a social contribution to the economic well-being of the country and the world. For this social contribution, John Jones today is given nothing . . . although he has a moral right to a share of the social wealth his work creates. We need a modification of the wage system, so that the worker may share in the profits, ownership or management of his industry. When labor leaders and capitalists thus agree together to give labor some capital to defend, there will no longer be two rival groups in industry; labor and management will become two cooperating members working together, as the two legs of a man cooperate to help him walk.

CHAPTER 15

Repose

NEVER before have men possessed so many time-saving devices. Never before have they had so little time for leisure or repose. Yet few of them are aware of this: advertising has created in modern minds the false notion that leisure and not-working are the same—that the more we are surrounded by bolts and wheels, switches and gadgets, the more time we have conquered for our own.

But this division of our days into working and not-working is too simple; in practice, for most men, it leaves out the very possibility of real leisure. They waste precious hours away from work in aimless loafing, in negative waiting-around for something interesting to come along.

True repose is not a mere intermission between the acts of the working-life. It is an intense activity, but of a different kind. Just as sleeping is not a cessation of life, but living of a different sort from wakefulness, so repose is an activity no less creative than that of our working hours.

Repose—true leisure—cannot be enjoyed without some recognition of the spiritual world. For the first purpose of repose is the contemplation of the good . . . its goal is a true perspective one, the small incidents of everyday life in their relation to the larger goodness that surrounds us. *Genesis* tells us that after the creation of the world, "*God saw all that he had made, and found it very good.*" Such contemplation of his work is natural to man, whenever he, too, is engaged in a creative task. The painter stands back from his canvas, to see whether the details of the seascape are properly placed. True repose is such a standing back to survey the activities that fill our days.

We cannot get a real satisfaction out of our work unless we pause, frequently, to ask ourselves why we are doing it, and whether its purpose is one our minds wholeheartedly approve. Perhaps one reason why so many of our economic and political projects miscarry is because they are in the hands of men with eyes so tightly glued to what they are doing that they never stop to question whether it should be done at all. Merely keeping busy, merely getting paid can never satisfy man's need for a creative work.

A job of any kind can be lifted up and given Divine purpose, if it is seen in the perspective of Eternity. The sweeping of a floor, the driving of a garbage-truck, the checking of a list of box-car numbers—all these can be "made good" through a simple act of the will which directs them to the service of God. The simplest task can be given spiritual significance and made divine.

If we direct our work towards God, we shall work better than we know. The admission of this fact is another of the tasks for which we need repose. Once a week man, reposing from work, does well to come before his God to admit how much of what he did during the week was the work of his Creator; he can remind himself, then, that the material on which he labored came from Other hands, that the ideas he employed entered his mind from a Higher source, that the very energy which he employed was a gift of God.

In such a mood of true repose, the scientist will see that he himself was not the author of his research volume on nature's laws, but only its proofreader. It was God who wrote the book. In such repose, the teacher will confess that every truth he passed on to his students was a ray from the sun of Divine Wisdom. The cook who peels potatoes after such a period of repose will handle them as humble gifts of God himself.

Repose allows us to contemplate the little things we do in their relationship to the vast things which alone can give them worth and meaning. It reminds us that all actions get their worth from God: "worship" means admitting "worth." To worship is to restore to our workaday life its true worth by setting it in its real relationship to God, who is its end and ours.

Such worship is a form of repose—of an intensely active and creative contemplation of Divine things, from which we arise refreshed. For the promise of the Gospel of St. Matthew is still waiting for those who are willing to hear it: *"Come to me, all you that labor and are burdened; I will give you rest."*

CHAPTER 16

The Idle in the Marketplace

A GREAT and distinguished psychologist once said that the tragedy of man today was that he no longer believed he had a soul to save. To such a group Our Lord addressed His beautiful parable of the laborers in the vineyard. Toward the close of the day the master of the vineyard went to the marketplace and said: "Why stand you here all the day idle?" In certain places of the East this custom still prevails, men gathering in front of Mosques and public places with shovels in their hands, waiting to be hired.

This story has a spiritual application and refers to various kinds of idlers. In addition to those who idle in the literal sense, there are mere loafers with nothing to do. Many are idle in the sense of being industrious triflers, wearied with toils that accomplish no real worth. Many are idle because of constant indecision, and others become frustrated and worried, not knowing the purpose of life. To the human eye, there are not many idlers, but as the Eye of Heaven looks down to earth it must be like a vast marketplace wherein few labor. To the Divine, all such activity as the acquiring of wealth, marrying and giving in marriage, buying and selling, studying and painting, are all means to the supreme and final end which is the saving of one's soul. Every expenditure of human strength which makes what is a means an end, which isolates living from the goal of living, is a busy idleness, a sad and mournful unreality.

Despite this new and harsh definition of idleness which Our Divine Lord gives, there is nevertheless much hope in the story, for some were hired at the eleventh hour, and they received just

THE IDLE IN THE MARKETPLACE

as much as those who had labored all the day. It is never too late for God's grace. It is a peculiar psychological fact that those who turn to God late in life generally consider all their previous life wasted. St. Augustine reflecting on his wasted youth said: "Too late, O ancient Beauty have I loved Thee." There are no hopeless cases; no life is too far spent to be recouped; no life long idleness precludes a few minutes of useful work in the vineyard of the Lord even the last few hours of life, as was the case with the penitent thief.

When the Lord gave everyone at the end of the day the same wages, those who had borne the heat and burdens of the sun complained that those who came in at the eleventh hour received just as much. To which Our Divine Lord retorted: "Does your eye see evil because I do good?" The thought of reward does not enter into the heavenly service. Those who lead a moral life for forty years and then protest the late-comers' salvation have the spirit of the hireling. With all the true acts of the spiritual man, the inspiration is love and not a desire of reward. One can not speak of the rewards of a true love in marriage without insulting the husband and wife. One can not associate compensation with the affection that twines a child's arms about a mother's neck, or that keeps her waiting in vigils that outwatch the patient stars. One can not associate reward with the heroism of a man who would risk his life to save another. In like manner the servitors of daily piety and religion are as full of the charm and fascination and glory of self-forgetting devotion as any of these.

Physical idleness deteriorates the mind; spiritual idleness deteriorates the heart. The joint action of air and water can turn a bar to rust. Therefore at every hour in the marketplace, man must ask himself: "Why stand I here idle?"

LOVE

CHAPTER 17

The Three Causes of Love

EVERY LOVE rests on a tripod. Every love has three bases or supports: goodness, knowledge and similarity.

Take *goodness* first: a man may be mistaken in his choice of what seems to him to be good, but he can never desire anything unless he believes in its intrinsic goodness. The prodigal son was seeking something good for him—something to satisfy his hunger —when he tried to live on husks; he was wrong only in his judgment, in thinking husks a fit food for a man. All of us are in the same predicament as he. We are forever trying to fill our lives, our minds, our bodies, our homes with "goods," and we accept nothing unless it seems, at the moment, to have some good in it. But our estimates are not always correct; we may mistake an apparent for a real good, thus injuring ourselves.

Without this reaching-out towards goodness, there would be no love: neither love of country, nor of pleasures, of friend, nor of spouse. Through loving, each heart tried to acquire a perfection which it lacks, or to express the perfection it already owns. All love springs out of goodness, for goodness, by its nature, is lovable to man.

The goodness which we love in other people is not always a moral goodness; it may be physical goodness, or utilitarian goodness. In such cases, an individual is loved because of the pleasure that he gives us, or because he is useful to us, or because he can "get it for us wholesale," or for some other reason in which selfishness is involved. But even then, there is a good we seek in our loving and unless something somehow seems good to us, we simply cannot care for it.

But *knowledge* is also involved in every love: We cannot love what we do not know. "Introduce me to her," is the phrase of a man who seeks the knowledge of a woman which, he knows, must precede the possibility of his really loving her. Even the "dream girl" of the bachelor has to be built up from fragments of knowledge in his mind. Hatred comes from want of knowledge, as love comes from knowledge; thus, bigotry is properly related to ignorance.

Knowledge, in the early stages, is a condition of love; but as the relationship deepens, love increases knowledge. A wife and husband who have lived together many years possess a new kind of knowledge of each other, deeper than any spoken word or any analysis of motives could provide. This knowledge (impossible in the honeymoon weeks) comes gradually from love-in-action, as a kind of intuitional understanding of what lies in the mind and heart of the other. It is thus possible for us to love beyond our knowledge, to allow faith to fill up the insufficiency of our intellectual understanding. A simple person in good faith may therefore have a greater love of God than a theologian, and this love can give him a keener understanding of the ways of God with human hearts than any psychologist will possess.

One of the reasons why decent people shrink from vulgar discussions of sex is that the knowledge two people gain of one another in so intimate a relation is, by its very nature, incommunicable to others. The whole exchange is so personal that those involved shrink from sharing it with outsiders—the knowledge thus gained is too sacred to be profaned. And it is a psychological fact that those whose theoretical knowledge of sex has been realized in the unifying love of marriage are least inclined to bring the matter out of its twilit realm of shared mystery to the glaring light of public discussion. This is not, at all, because they are "disillusioned" about sex, but because sex has now been changed by the transcendent alchemy of love, so that its nature can no longer be understood by those who stand outside the shared experience. On the other hand those whose knowledge of sex has not been sublimated into the mystery of love (and who are therefore frustrated) are the ones who like to talk about sex. Husbands and wives whose marriages are marred by infidelity seek such discussions; fathers and mothers who are happy in their relation never want to mention it.

When knowledge has been transmuted to love, it fills the heart so full that no outsider could contribute anything further, and the matter need never be aired. People who talk about their intimate relations confess, by doing so, that they have not raised their love high enough to turn it into a mystery, or transformed it into the only kind of love between the sexes that deserves the name.

The third leg of the tripod on which love rests is *similarity*: similarity between two persons, leading to love, need not indicate that they are both alike in actual fact. It can mean merely that one possesses in actuality what the other owns potentially. Because the human heart, itself imperfect, desires perfection, we seek, through love, to make up for our own deficiencies. The homely young man will wish to marry a beautiful girl: the potential beauty (which he does not possess himself, but for which he has a hunger) attracts him to that which is beautiful beyond himself.

Similarity underlies even the most vulgar and tawdry of our loves. The woman who is a social climber cultivates "important" people because they possess, in actuality, what she would like to have, but lacks. On a much higher level, saints love sinners— not because they share developed qualities of soul, but because the saint is able to apprehend the possible virtue in the sinner. It was thus that the Son of God Himself became the Son of man: He loved what man might be and, in the words of St. Augustine, "He became man that man might become like God."

CHAPTER 18

When Lovers Fail
There Is Love

MARRIAGES FAIL when love is regarded not as something transparent like a window pane which looks out on the heavens, but as something opaque like a curtain which sees nothing beyond the human. When couples do not see that the love of the flesh is the preface to the love of the spirit, one of the partners is often made the object of worship in place of God. This is the essence of idolatry, the worship of the image of the reality; the mistaking of the copy for the original, and the frame for the picture.

Human love promises something only God can give. When God is ignored in love, the one who was worshipped as a deity is discovered not to be a God, or even an angel. Because he or she did not give all that was promised, being incapable of giving it, because not Divine, the other feels betrayed, deceived, disappointed and cheated. The stem of the rose is blamed for not bearing what it could not bear, the marble bust of deity. The result is that erotic love turns to hate when the other is discovered to have feet of clay—to be a woman instead of an angel, to be a man instead of an Apollo. When the ecstasy does not continue, and the band stops playing, and the champagne of life loses its sparkle, the other partner is called a cheat and a robber. And then finally called to a divorce court on the grounds of incompatibility.

Then begins the search for a new partner, on the assumption that some other human being can supply what only God can give. Instead of seeing that the basic reason for the failure of marriage was the refusal to use married love as the vestibule of the Divine, one thinks that husks can satisfy, when one was meant to eat only the bread of angels. The very fact that a man or a woman seeks a new partner is a proof that there never was any love at all, for though sex is replaceable, love is not. Sex is for a pleasure; love is for a person.

Cows can graze on other pastures, but a person admits of no substitution. As soon as a person becomes equated with a package to be judged only by its wrappings, it will not be long when the tinsel turns green and the package will be discarded. This arrangement enslaves a woman, because she is much more a creature of time than man, and her security becomes less and less through the years. She is always much more concerned about her age than a man, and thinks more of marriage in terms of time. This is because a man is afraid of dying before he has lived, but a woman is basically afraid of dying before she has begotten life. A woman wants the fulfillment of life more than a man, and it is less the experience of life that she craves, than the prolongation of life. Whenever the laws and the customs of a country permit an arrangement whereby a woman can be discarded because she has dishpan hands, it ends by making her the slave not of dishpans but of man.

Life is not a snare nor an illusion. It would be that only if there were no Infinite to satisfy our yearnings. Everyone wants a Love that will never die and one that has no moments of hate or satiety. That Love lies beyond humans.

Human love is a spark from the great flame of Eternity. The happiness which comes from the unity of two in one flesh is a prelude to that greater communion of two in one spirit. In this way, marriage becomes a tuning fork to the song of the angels, or a river that runs to the sea. Then it is evident that there is an answer to the elusive mystery of love and that somewhere there is a reconciliation of the quest and the goal, and that is in final union with God, where the chase and the capture, the romance and the marriage fuse into one. For since God is boundless, Eternal Love, it will take an ecstatic eternal chase to sound its depths.

CHAPTER 19

True Love

THERE ARE TWO KINDS of love: love for its own pleasure, or love for the sake of another; the first is carnal love, the second is spiritual. Carnal love knows the other person only in a biological moment. Spiritual love knows the other person at all moments. In erotic love, the burdens of the other are regarded as impairing one's own happiness; in spiritual love, the burdens of others are opportunities for service.

Somewhere along the line, the modern world has been duped and fooled into giving the name of love to some vague obsession which parades itself in every billboard advertisement, reigns in the film industry, puzzles dramatists who must solve triangles short of suicide, makes novels best sellers, perfumes so exotic as to be unfit for a tyro's concupiscence, and humor more spicy. Love has become so vulgarized, so carnalized, that those who really love are almost afraid to use the word. It is used now almost exclusively to describe one of the opposite sex, rather than a person; it is made to revolve around glands, rather than a will, and is centered in biology instead of personality. Even when it disguises itself as infatuation for another, it is nothing else than a desire to intensify its own self-centeredness.

Purely human love is the embryo of the Love of the Divine. One finds some suggestions of this in Plato, who argues that the purpose of love is to make the first step toward religion. He pictures love for beautiful persons being transformed into love for beautiful souls, then into a love of justice, goodness and finally God who is their source. Erotic love is, therefore, a bridge which one crosses, not a buttress where one sits and rests; it is not an airport but an airplane; it is always going somewhere else, upwards and onwards. All carnal love presupposes incompleteness, deficiency, yearning for completion, and an attraction for enrichment, for all love is a flight for immortality. There is a suggestion of Divine Love in every form of erotic love, as the lake reflects the moon. The only reason there is love for creatures in human hearts, is that it may lead to the love of the Creator. As food is for the body, as body is for the soul, as the material is for the spiritual, so the flesh is for the eternal. That is why in the language of human love, there can often be detected the language of Divinity, such as "worship," "angel," "adore."

The Saviour did not crush and then extinguish the flames that burned in Magdalene's heart, but transfigured them to a new object of affection. The Divine commendation that was given to the woman who poured out the ointment on the feet of her Saviour, reminded her that love which once sought its own pleasure can be transmuted into a love that will die for the beloved. For that reason He referred to His burial at the very moment her thoughts were closest to life.

Because it is in the Divine plan to use the love of the flesh as a stepping stone to the love of the Divine, it always happens in a well regulated moral heart, that as time goes on, the erotic love diminishes, and the religious love increases. That is why in true marriages the love of God increases through the years, not in the sense that husband and wife love one another less, but that they love God more. Love passes from an affection for outer appearances, to those inner depths of personality which embody the Divine Spirit.

There are few things more beautiful in life than to see that deep passion of man for woman which begot children as the mutual incarnation of their love, transfigured into that deeper "passionless passion and wild tranquility" which is God.

CHAPTER 20

The Effects of Want of Love

MOST PEOPLE in the world are unloved. Some do not make themselves lovable because of their selfishness; others do not have enough Christian spirit to love those who do not love them. The result is that the world is full of lonely hearts. Here we speak not of love in the romantic or carnal sense, but in the higher sense of generosity, forgiveness, kindness and sacrifice. Perhaps it would help some to know some of the psychological effects of not loving others in a really noble and unselfish way.

The first effect of not receiving love because one is generous and loving toward others is cynicism and even hostility. Never a good word can be said for anyone. Because one is unloved one tries to make everyone else unlovable. Characters are assassinated, the noblest motives reduced to the basest, and slanders believed and propagated. When others do show them kindness they look "for the catch in it"; even gifts are viewed with suspicion and the sincerest of compliments acknowledged with a charge of insincerity. Because such egotists are so miserable they seek to make everyone else miserable. Never once do they see that they are the cause of their own unhappiness. Someone else is always to blame. "I bumped into the other car, because *you* made me nervous this morning at breakfast by asking about my bank balance." "I have a cold now because you did not give me a mink coat like the wives of the other officials have."

And the effect of want of love is the martyrdom complex, which is a morbid attempt to get pity or sympathy when real love is gone. Feigning sickness is one of the tricks. Because good health does not win the affection of others, one pretends to be wounded in the firm hope that someone else will bind the wounds. The "pain" which is in the mind is loss of love. That "pain" is translated into the body and becomes sickness. If one could put into words what goes on inside of such a person it might be this: "I really want to be well. But if I become sick, then others *must* love me." Just as headaches can be caused by a desire to escape responsibility, so disease can be caused by a desire to win affection. This reaches a point in some where they become bed-ridden for years or unable to walk. In the San Francisco earthquake it was said that over thirty people who had not walked in over a period of twenty years, got up and walked. These were mental, not physical cripples.

Another type of reaction is in those who admit that they need love, but say: "I will pretend from now on that I do not need it." As a result they develop a false spirit of independence, become quarrelsome, oppose every idea and suggestion regardless of how good it is, develop anti-social instincts, smoke in front of no-smoking signs, and park in front of no-parking signs. Hardness and roughness and a certain toughness and boorishness of character is many times nothing other than a bold front for want of love.

It is very likely that the over-emphasis on security in society today is due to a want of love. In other generations people wanted to be happy, and many of them were happy in the framework both of a family and of a permanent marriage bond, or in the embrace of religion. Now the instability of the home through divorce is increasing. A substitute must be found for married love, and it comes out in a ruthless quest for power and security which is only one of the lesser ingredients of happiness. The business man who is completely lost in his business and stays at the office late hours rather than go home may sometimes be doing that to compensate for his want of love at home. Some doctors are now tracing some skin diseases to mental causes. It has been said that some people who are afraid to "face the world" develop skin blemishes. A "Stained mind" becomes a "stained body." Whatever be the medical evidence to support this view, it is true that no group of women seem to have complexions like nuns. Most of them never look into a mirror, but they have one incomparably fine beauty aid which many other people lack, namely, a good conscience and peace of soul. The skin of those who suffer with a hidden sense of guilt almost tells the story of the diseases going on inside the soul. One person who had repressed guilt and kept saying to herself: "I am a moral leper," developed a skin infection which vanished when reconciliation was made with her husband.

There is no cure for want of love but love. There will always be love for the lovable, but there will never be love for the unlovable unless we begin to love them for God's sake. Thus we are brought back again to religion and to God whose New Testament definition of His essence is: "God is love."

CHAPTER 21

The Infinite and Sex

O_{F ALL} the things man knows, the thing he knows least about is himself. He is forever trying to solve the riddle of himself, to prove the meaning of his nature. Some modern writers attempt to find a short-cut solution by reducing man to a single one of his many instincts: sex. Appalled at the difficulty of understanding the whole man, they blot out of consciousness all of him except one tiny area and, by studying that, pretend that they have charted man. This "answer" gains popularity with those who have lost an understanding of the true goal of life: not knowing their proper end, they cling to the intensity of sensual experiences and use them as a drug by which they may escape from worry over the ultimate meaning of their lives.

Sex is a small part of men, but it always affords a bridge to the infinite, the supernatural: if it is not divinized by selfless love, it becomes diabolically perverse. Man cannot be a "mere animal," as the animals are. To the young, whose sexual desires are strongest, infinity is the normal climate of the mind. Young men live in dreams and hopes of the future, and all their desires are infinite in their scope, so that false mysticism is very close to every youthful urge: whatever the young man feels is so intensely felt that he can set no bounds to it. "Calf-love" is no exception to the rule.

Even among those who deny God, sex remains one matter which can never be taken for granted. Their very shame, or denial of shame, implies that this instinct is one which involves the spirit, as other instincts do not. No one ever blushes over his desire to eat, even when his hunger is intense—yet all men blush if they are accused of being secretly in love. They intuitively feel that there is something sacred and secretive about this passion, so that it should not be bruited about too carelessly: it involves secrets only Heaven should know. That is why marriage, even among savages, has always been surrounded by religious rites.

The spirit cannot be banned from sex. The human wish for fidelity and love that lasts, for loyalty and for true devotion do not spring from the flesh, but from the spirit of man. Sex thus acts as a link between the worlds of spirit and of matter. Shame enters in to protect the spiritual aspect from being detected by the coarse hands of the world. And it is through the spirit that men are allies of infinity.

Love, which properly is both the origin and goal of sex, is infinite in another way: it is meant to be outgoing, radiating from the small center of self to limitless distances. Love is centrifugal; it flees the ego and seeks its object in God and all His children who come our way. Love is something we can never hoard, something that must be spent to be possessed. In the family, this is splendidly exemplified, for the love, which first exists between husband and wife alone, grows greater as it is further expended by both upon their children and one another.

Once given, love should never be taken back, according to God's scheme. It is meant to push out from us, farther and farther into His infinite, until we love all things because we see them as His Own. But if sex is separated from love, and made mere means of self-gratification, the process is unhealthily reversed. The other person is now seen as a mere means to pleasure, not as a person commanding love. The "affair" becomes a mere exchange of egotistical delights. And, since love was never meant to be recalled, to summon it back upon the self in such a way turns it to poison, makes it a burden on the heart, transforms its energy to hate. The centripetal movement of love . . . from the neighbor and God towards the ego . . . means frustration, hate and worry. God can come to us through anyone we love, so long as our love for him is outgoing, is concerned with his best interests and not our own. But sexual activity that is egotistic destroys our relationship to God and neighbor. The infinite is always entered through the gate of self-forgetfulness by means of love; to turn back towards self again is to revert to the infinite and the discontentment that accompanies all efforts to find happiness by self-indulgence.

Sex is the most "psychosomatic" of human functions: there is nothing else in which body and soul, finite and infinite, flesh and spirit are so closely intertwined. When sex is allowed to link the two, peace and joy result; when the flesh and spirit are divorced, and sex is sought alone, boredom and ennui result. It is life's long task to keep the relationship of soul and body in their proper order. A sex philosophy which, ignoring this necessity, encourages one to love the *body* of another, dooms love; for it is only if the object of our love is *body-plus-soul* that love can last. It is the Infinite beyond them both which enables a man and a woman to remain in love. If they attempt to leave the spirit out . . . to limit their love affair to a mere Thou and I . . . there is no love. For either the Thou becomes absorbed in the I (which is power and seduction) or the I is surrendered to the Thou (which is idolatry). Two full and loving personalities can love only if they invite the blessing of the Infinite, of God.

CHAPTER 22

Reflections on Love

THE EGO has a peculiar way of disguising the real reasons of its love. It can pretend to be interested in another's welfare while actually it is seeking its own pleasure.

There are some people who love to boast of their tolerance, but actually it is inspired by egotism; they want to be left alone in their own ideas, however wrong they be, so they plead for a tolerance of other people's ideas. But this kind of tolerance is very dangerous, for it becomes intolerance as soon as the ego is disturbed or menaced. That is why a civilization which is tolerant about false ideas instead of being charitable to persons is on the eve of a great wave of intolerance and persecution.

The egotist always considers his ego in terms of not having or wanting something. His principle action is drawing something to himself like the mouth which absorbs food. There is no out-going, no service, and never a sacrifice, because he interprets sacrifice as the diminishing of himself.

True love, on the contrary, feels that the need to give is more imperious than the need to receive. At the beginning of love there is a feeling that one can never give enough. Regardless of how precious the gift, it still seems to fall short of what one would offer. Price tags are torn off, because we want no proportion established between the gift and the need of giving. The tragedy of love when it begins to die, is that then people do not even give what they have. No longer is there a question of not being able to give enough; there is rather no giving at all.

In real love there is pity and need. Pity in the sense that one feels the need of expansion and of giving to the point of exhaustion; need, because of a void that one would see filled. True love receives without ever interpreting what is given. It never seeks another motive than that of love itself. He who asks "Why" something is given does not trust.

One of the tragedies of our time is that freedom is interpreted in terms of freedom *from* something instead of in terms of love. The man who loves everybody is the free man; the man who hates is the man who has already enslaved himself. The man who hates is dependent on that which he cannot love—and therefore he is not free. To hate one's next door neighbor is a restriction of freedom. It demands walking around the block so one will not see him, or waiting until he leaves the house before leaving oneself.

It is our loves and desires that determine our pains. If our supreme love is the pleasure of the body, then our greatest pain is loss of health; if our supreme love is wealth, then our deepest worry is insecurity; if our supreme love is God, then our greatest fear is sin.

The great mystery is not why we love, but why we are loved. It is easy to understand why we love because of our incompleteness and our radical dissatisfaction apart from goodness. But why anyone should love us is the mystery, for we know when we look at our real selves how very little there is to love. Why creatures should love us is not too great a mystery, for they are imperfect too. But for God to love us—that we will never understand. The soul that has finally come to love God is worried by the thought that he has already lost so much time. As St. Augustine said: "Too late, O ancient Beauty have I loved Thee." But, on the other hand, this regret is compensated for by the knowledge that it was always in the Divine plan that we should eventually come to know God.

We love to see ourselves idealized in the minds of others. That is one of the beautiful joys of love. We become fresh, innocent, brave, strong in the mind of the beloved. Love covers up the corruption of the soul. The winter of discontent is forgotten by being clothed in the blossoms of a new spring. After a while the lover begins to substitute what he really is in his own mind, with what he is in the mind of the other. It is this idealization which pleases in love. That is why love gives an incentive to betterment. When the other thinks well of us, we try to be worthy of that opinion. The fact that others assume us to be good is a great incentive to goodness. That is why too, one of the basic principles of life ought to be to assume goodness in others; thus we make them good.

CHAPTER 23

The Mystery of Love

THERE COMES A MOMENT in even the noblest of human loves when the mystery has gone. One has now grown "used to" the best, and has come to take it for granted, as jewelers may casually handle the most precious stones without troubling to admire them. What we completely possess, we can no longer desire. What we have already attained, we cannot hope for. Yet hope and desire and, above all, mystery, are needed to keep our interest in life alive.

When wonder has vanished from our days, then they become banal. Our minds were made to function at the stretch and to reach out, forever, towards the solution of some lofty problem that forever eludes us. It is possible that the popularity of mystery novels in our day is occasioned by the fact that so many people have ceased to dwell on the mysteries of faith and are looking, in any cheap substitute that comes to hand, for something to replace what they have lost. Readers of mystery stories spend all their wonder on the method by which someone was killed; they do not, as the contemporaries of Dante and of Michaelangelo would have done, wonder about the eternal fate of those who die.

Man cannot be happy if he is satiated; our zest comes from the fact that there are doors not yet opened, veils not yet lifted, notes that have not been struck. If a "love" is only physical, marriage will bring the romance to an end: the chase is ended, and the mystery is solved. Whenever any person is thus taken for granted, there is a loss of the sensitivity and delicacy which are the essential condition of friendship, joy and love in human relations. Marriage is no exception; one of its most tragic outcomes is mere possession without desire.

There is no love left when one hits bottom, or imagines that he has; the personality we have exhausted of its mystery is a bore. There must be always something unrevealed, some mystery we have not probed, some passion that we cannot glut . . . and this is true even in the arts. We do not want to hear a singer constantly reiterate her highest note, nor have an orator tear a passion to tatters.

In a true marriage there is an ever-deepening mystery and, therefore, an ever-enchanting romance. At least four of the mysteries of marriage can be tabulated. First comes the mystery of the other partner's physical being, the mystery of sex. When that mystery has been solved, and the first baby is born, a new mystery begins: the husband sees in his wife a thing he never saw before—the beautiful mystery of motherhood. She sees in him the sweet mystery of fatherhood. As other children come to revive their strength and beauty, the husband never seems older to his wife than on the day they met, and the wife appears to him as freshly beautiful as when they first became engaged.

When the children reach the age of reason, a third mystery unfolds: that of mother-craft and father-craft—the disciplining of young minds and hearts in the ways of God. As the children grow to maturity this mystery continues to deepen; each child's personality is something for the parents to explore and then to form closer to the likeness of the God of love.

The fourth mystery of the happily married involves their social living, the contribution that they jointly make to the well-being of the world. Here lies the root of democracy, for in the family the individual is not valued for what he is worth, nor for what he can do, but for what he is. His status, his position in the home, is granted him by virtue of merely being alive. If a child is dumb or blind, if a son has been maimed at the war, he is still loved for himself and for his intrinsic worth as a child of God. No parent mitigates his love because of changes in a child's earning power or worldly wisdom, or troubles about the class to which his off-spring may belong. This reverence for personality for its own sake in the family is the social principle on which the wider life of the community depends and is a potent reminder of the most important of all political principles: the state exists for the person, and not the person for the state.

CHAPTER 24

Love and Ecstasy

Ecstasy means to be "carried out of oneself" and, broadly speaking, the very fact of loving carries the lover out of himself by leading him to center his thoughts, beyond himself, on the beloved. Adolescent boys and girls are often surprised to find that their elders know they have fallen in love; they give themselves away by their dreamy inattention, by staring into space and by indifference to such things as meal-times. Love has "carried them away."

Love, again, is at the bottom of all the stories about the absent-minded professors, who, on rainy nights, put the umbrella to bed and stand themselves in the sink; the things of the mind they love have "carried them out" of their surroundings. Any great love has a similar effect: it makes the lover indifferent to physical hardships and sordid surroundings. The hovel of a man and wife who love each other is a far more joyous place than the rich apartment of the couple who have lost their love. Love of God begets an even greater indifference to our environment: a saint like St. Vincent de Paul was so carried away by his love for God's poor that he forgot to feed himself. As Edna St. Vincent Millay wrote of the Christian life: "If you pitch your tent each evening nearer the town of your true desire, and glimpse its gates less far, then you lay you down on nettles, you lay you down with vipers, and you scarcely notice where you are."

But there is one great difference between human love and the love of God, although both of them "carry us away." In human love, the ecstasy comes at the beginning. But when it is a matter of loving God, the ecstasy is attained only after one has passed through much suffering and agony of soul. In bodily enjoyments, we encounter first the feast and then the fast, and maybe the headache, as well. But the spirit encounters first the fast, and perhaps the headache, only as a necessary prelude to the feast. The ecstatic pleasures enjoyed by a young husband and wife at the commencement of their marriage are, in a sense, a "bait," inducing them to fulfill their mission of parenthood. The honeymoon is a kind of Divine credit extended to those who, later on, will have to pay the costs of rearing a family. But no great ecstasy, either of the spirit or of the flesh, is given us as a permanent possession without our having to pay for it. Every ecstasy carries a price tag with it.

"First fervor is false fervor" in marriage as in religion. The earliest ecstasy is not the true, lasting love we seek to find and hold. That may come to us—but only after many purging trials, fidelities under stress, perseverance through discouragement and a steady pursuit of our Divine destiny past all the allurements of this earth. The deep, ecstatic love of some Christian fathers and mothers is a beautiful thing to see: but they have won it after passing through their Calvaries. Theirs is the true ecstasy, which belongs less to youth than to old age.

The first ecstasy of love is a thrill, but a somewhat selfish thrill: in it, the lover seeks to get from the beloved all that he will give. In the second ecstasy, he tries to receive from God all that both of them can give. If love is identified with the early ecstasy alone, it will seek its prolongation in another person's presence; if it is identified with a unifying, enduring and eternal love, it will seek the deepening of its mystery in the Divine, Who put all loves into our hearts.

Too many husbands and wives expect their partners in marriage to give what only God can give: eternal ecstasy. Yet if any man or woman could do that, he would be God. We are right to want the ecstasy of love; but if we expect to enjoy it through the flesh, which is merely on pilgrimage to God, we prepare ourselves for disappointment. The first ecstasy of love is not an illusion; but it is only a kind of travel-folder, a foretaste, a preview, urging body and soul to start the journey towards eternal joys. If the first ecstasy passes, this change is not an invitation to love another person, but to love in another way—and the other way is the Christ Way, the way of Him Who said: "I am the Way."

CHILDREN

CHAPTER 25

Motherhood

Human motherhood is twofold in its essence, and is a more complex thing than motherhood among the animals. There is, first, the physical act of giving birth, which women share with all of nature. As the tree bears fruit and the hen hatches her eggs, so every mother, by the act of birth, is bound up with the life of all living things, and of her it may be rightly said, "Blessed is the fruit of thy womb."

But human motherhood has a second and far lordlier aspect—that of the spirit. The soul of a child does not emanate from the mother's soul or body, but is freshly created by God Himself, Who infuses it into the body of the unborn child. Physiological motherhood is glorified by this co-operation with God Himself, Who fathered the baby's soul and then permitted a woman to clothe it in her flesh. The human mother does not bear a mere animal but *a man,* made to the image and likeness of the God Who created him.

Every child born of woman has, then, two fathers: his earthly father, without whom he could not have life, and his Heavenly Father, without Whom he could not possess a personality, a soul, an irreplaceable "I." The mother is the essential partner through whom both fathers work. Her own relationship to the child has two resulting aspects: there is the mother-baby aspect, wherein the child is physically and almost absolutely dependent on the mother. But there is also the mother-person relationship (expressed at baptism, when the child is given its own name). This confirms the dignity and separate selfhood of even the smallest infant and foreshadows his right eventually to lead his own life and to depart from his parents to cling to a wife of his own.

Every birth requires a submission and a disciplining. The earth itself must undergo harrowing before it passively accepts the seed. In woman, the submission is not passive: it is sacrificial, consciously creative, and for this selflessness her whole nature has been formed. It is well known that women are capable of far more sustained sacrifice than men; a man may be a hero in a crisis, and then slip back to mediocrity. He lacks the moral endurance which enables a woman to be heroic through the years, months, days and even seconds of her life, when the very repetitive monotony of her tasks wears down the spirit. Not only a woman's days, but her nights—not only her mind, but her body must share in the Calvary of motherhood. That is why women have a surer understanding of the doctrine of redemption than men have: they have come to associate the risk of death with life in childbirth, and to understand the sacrifice of self to another through the many months preceding it.

In a mother two of the great spiritual laws are united into one: love of neighbor and co-operation with God's grace—and both of them are applied in a unique way. For love of neighbor, to anyone except a mother, is love of a nonself; a mother's neighbor during pregnancy is one with herself, yet to be loved differently from the self. The sacrifice sometimes involved in neighborly love now takes place within her flesh: the agent and the object of her sacrifice are both contained within her.

And the co-operation with grace in a mother, although it may be unconscious on her part, yet makes her a partner of Divinity: every human mother is, in a sense, "over-shadowed by the Holy Ghost." Not a priest, and yet endowed with a kind of priestly power, she, too, brings God to man, and man to God. She brings God to man by accepting her mother's role, and thus permitting God to infuse a new soul into her body for it to bear. She brings man to God in childbirth itself, when she allows herself to be used as an instrument by which another child of God is born into the world.

If motherhood is seen as a matter involving only a woman and a man it is seen too astigmatically, and without the honor that is its due. For to comprehend the real significance of motherhood, we must include the spiritual element that goes to make a child—we must see the human woman co-operating with her husband, the father of the human baby, and with God, the Father of a soul that is eternal, indestructible and unlike any other ever formed throughout the history of the world. Thus every human motherhood involves a partnership with the Divine.

CHAPTER 26

Parents and Children

THERE ARE NO juvenile delinquents; there are only delinquent parents. The Fourth Commandment, "Honor thy father and thy mother," is hardly ever quoted today as the means of restoring domestic peace. If discipline in the home is neglected, it is rarely made up for later. As Coleridge said: "If you bring up your children in a way which puts them out of sympathy with the religious feelings of the nations in which they live, the chances are that they will ultimately turn out ruffians and fanatics, and one as likely as the other." The effects of the conduct of children on their parents vary. Mothers suffer more at their evil ways than fathers enjoy their good ways.

The duty of parents to children is to rule while avoiding exasperating severity on the one hand and excessive indulgences on the other. God gives parents a child as so much plastic material that can be molded for good or evil. What if God placed a precious diamond in the hands of parents and told them to inscribe on it a sentence which would be read on the Last Day, and shown as an index of their thoughts and ideals? What caution they would exercise in their selection! And yet the example parents give their children will be that by which they will be judged on the Last Day. This tremendous responsibility never means that parents, when their children do wrong, should provoke them to wrath, for wrath leads to discouragement. Parents hold the place of God in the house. If they act as tyrants they will develop unconsciously anti-religious sentiments in their children. Children love approbation and can be easily cast down into despair when blamed excessively for trivial faults. With great difficulty can children ever be taught the Love and Mercy of God, if His vice regents in the home act without it and are so difficult to please. When good intentions are rated low, and children are put under the ban of dishonor, they are likely to show they are no better than their parents think they are.

Children came into their own with Christianity when its Divine Founder said: "Suffer the little children to come unto Me, and forbid them not for such is the Kingdom of Heaven." He consecrated childhood by becoming a child, playing on the green hills of Nazareth and watching the mother eagles stir among their young. From that day it became eternally true: "Train up the child in the way he should go; and when he is old he will not depart from it." As the twig is bent, so is the tree. It is interesting, when one sees children, to speculate from the way they act as to the kind of homes from which they come. As one can judge the vitality of a tree from the fruit it produces, so one can tell the character of the parents from their children. One knows that from certain homes there will never be an errant child, while a glance at a mother or father will reveal a future full of fears for the child.

The present tendency is to shift responsibility to the school. But it must be remembered that education will make as much difference to a child as soil and air and sunshine do. A seed will grow better in one soil and climate than in another, but the kind of tree that grows depends on the kind of seed that is sowed. Then too, one must inquire if education is of the mind alone, or also of the will. Knowledge is in the mind; character is in the will. To pour knowledge into the mind of a child, without disciplining his will to goodness, is like putting a rifle into the hands of a child. Without education of the mind a child could be a stupid devil. With education of the mind, but without love of goodness, a child could grow up to be a clever devil.

The nation of tomorrow is the youth of today. They are the assurance of progress; the fresh arrows to a better future; the wings of aspiration. Even in war the strength of a nation is not in its bombs, but in the soldiers who defend it. In peace, it is not economics or politics that save, but good economists and good politicians—but to be that, they must be good children. To be that, there must in the first place be the grace of God; in the second place, in the home lessons of love and truth; in the schools, knowledge and self-control. Even in their early failures, the parents are not to be discouraged, remembering that fifteen centuries ago when the heart of a mother was broken for her wanton boy, St. Ambrose said to her: "Fear not, Monica; the child of so many tears cannot perish." That vain and wanton boy grew up to be the great and learned St. Augustine, whose "Confessions" everyone ought to read before he dies.

YOUTH

CHAPTER 27

Blood, Sweat and Tears

RECENTLY a woman at a Forum asked an important politician this question: "Why is it that our political leaders never speak of blood, sweat, tears and sacrifice, but only of how much they will give the farmers and the manufacturers and the labor unions if they are elected?" The politician answering quoted another politician, but it seemed as if he missed the deep significance of the woman's question. Actually, she was a spokesman of a large segment of the American people who know enough about history and psychology to know that no nation, as an individual, ever achieves anything worth while except through sacrifice and self-denial.

Toynbee pointed out that sixteen out of nineteen civilizations which have decayed from the beginning of history to the present, have rotted from within; only three fell to attacks from without. Very often an attack from the outside solidifies a nation and strengthens its moral fibers. Lincoln once said he never feared that America would be conquered from without, but that it might fall from within. Lenin once said that America would collapse by spending itself to death, an eventuality that is not too distant with a national debt of a little less than three hundred billion dollars.

Was Walter Whitman speaking of our age as well as his own when he wrote: "Society in these days is cankered, crude, superstitious and rotten . . . Genuine belief seems to have left us. . . . The great cities reek with respectable as well as non-respectable robbery and scoundrels. In fashionable life, flippancy, tepid amours, weak infidelities, small aims, or no aims at all, only to kill time. . . . It is as if we were somehow endowed with a vast and thoroughly appointed body, but then left with little or no soul."

Whitman's worry was in the woman's mind for she was disturbed about our indifference, tepidity and moral apathy. If there is anything that is becoming clear in our national life, it is that so-called progressive education is extremely unprogressive. Juvenile delinquency, crime, racketeering, political scandals—all these illegitimate children are dropped on the door step of an educational theory that denied a distinction between right and wrong and assumed that self-restraint was identical with the destruction of personality. Every instinct and impulse in either a child or an adult, does not, if left to itself, necessarily produce good results. Man has a hunting instinct which is good when directed to deer in season, but bad when directed to the police in season or out of season. The disrespect for authority which is the outgrowth of the stupidity that every individual is his own determinant of right and wrong has now become an epidemic of lawlessness.

Someday our educators will awaken to several basic facts about youth: 1) Youth has an intellect and a will. The intellect is the source of his knowledge; the will the source of his decisions. If his choices are wrong, the youth will be wrong regardless of how much he knows. 2) Education through the communication of knowledge does not necessarily make a good man; it can conceivably make learned devils instead of stupid devils. 3) Education is successful when it trains the mind to see the right targets, and disciplines the will to choose them rather than the wrong targets.

At present two currents manifest themselves in our American way of life: one is in the direction of a great development of moral character both in individuals and in the nation; the other is toward the surrender of morality and responsibility through a socialist state in which there will be no morality but state-morality, no conscience but state-conscience. Of the two the first is by far the stronger, though neither politics nor economics has seen it. Some of our educators are turning away from the spoiled child psychology, in which the child was called progressive if he did whatever he wanted; now the return is toward doing a little bit of thinking and working in order to wrest us out of our juvenile delinquency and moral flabbiness.

Youth particularly is yearning for something hard; it no longer believes its teachers who say that good or evil is a point of view and it makes no difference in which you believe. They now want to believe that something is so evil that we ought to fight against it, and something is so good that we ought, if necessary, to steel and discipline ourselves and even die to defend it. This latent power of blood and sweat and tears in our American youth will be captured within the next generation by one of the other forces: either by some political crackpot who will turn that desire for sacrifice into something like Nazism, Fascism or Communism, or by our leaders, political, educational and moral who will first show self-discipline and moral courage in their own lives and thus give an example to others.

The greatest responsibility falls on religious leaders whose message ought to be the message the woman wanted from politicians —the clarion call to restraint on evil influences and the showing forth of altruism and love of God.

The Teen-Agers

ADOLESCENCE, or "teen-age," is the short hour between the springtime and the summer of life. Before the teen-age is reached, there is very little individuality or personality, but as soon as the teens begin, the emotional life takes on the character of its environment, like water takes its shape from the vessel into which it is poured. The adolescent begins to be conscious of himself and others, and for that reason begins to live in solitude. The youth is more lonely than many parents and teachers know; perhaps the teen-ager agonizes in a greater solitariness of spirit than at any other time in life until maturity when the sense of unrequited guilt begins to weigh down the human soul.

As the teen-ager projects his personality to the world round about him, he seems to get further away from it. Between his soul and the world there seems to be a wall. There is never a complete self-analysis. As it takes an infant a long time to coordinate his eyes and his hands, so it takes the teen-ager a long time to adjust himself completely to this great broad world to which he feels so strangely related. He cannot yet take it in stride; novelty, new emotional experiences, great dreams and hopes flood his soul, each demanding attention and satisfaction. He does not confide his emotional states to others; he just lives. It is hard for the adult to penetrate the shell into which the teen-ager crawls. Like Adam after his fall, he hides from discovery.

Along with this loneliness, there goes a great desire to be noticed, for egotism is a vice that has to be mastered early in youth. This craving for attention accounts for the loudness in manner of some teen-agers. Not only does it attract the gaze of others, but it also experiences a latent sense of rebellion against others, and affirms that he is living for himself in his own way and as he pleases.

Along with this quality of inpenetrability the teen-ager becomes an imitator almost like the Japanese. Being in rebellion against the fixed and being governed largely by fleeting impressions, he becomes like a chameleon, which takes on the colors of the objects upon which it is placed. He becomes a hero or a bandit, a saint or a thief, depending on the environment or his reading or his companions. This spirit of imitation reveals itself in the dress. Overalls, shirts sticking out of trousers and overhanging like the flag of a defeated army, hair cuts fashioned after the savages of Oceania—all these become universal among youths who are afraid to march "against the grain."

There are few natural leaders among teen-agers, most of them being content to follow others. In this unconscious mimicry of others is a moral danger, for character is dependent on the ability to say "No". Unless education can give to teen-agers a training of the will, many of them will slip into adulthood and become slaves of propaganda and public opinion the rest of their lives. Instead of creating, they imitate. To create is to recognize the spirit in things; to imitate is to submerge personality at the lowest level of the mass.

Elders must not be too critical of the teen-agers, particularly when they rebel against them. From one point of view they are not in rebellion against restraint, but against their elders for not giving them a goal and purpose of life. The teen-ager's protest is not conscious. He does not know why he hates his parents, why he is rebellious against authority, why his fellow teen-agers are becoming more and more delinquent. But the real reason is under the surface; it is an unconscious protest against a society which has not given him a pattern of life. The schools he attends have never stressed restraint, discipline or self-control. Many of the teachers have defined freedom and even democracy as the right to do whatever you please. When this temporary phase of rebellion is past, the teen-agers will look for some great cause to which they can make a total dedication. They must have an ideal. In many instances today, they have no greater object of worship than to wrap their emotional lives around a movie hero, a movie star, a band leader or a crooner. This sign of decaying civilizations will pass when the catastrophe comes. Then youth will look for a different type to imitate, namely, either heroes or saints. A sad commentary it is on our civilization that the teen-agers have never rallied around our war heroes. This is because they are not yet ready for the more solid ideal. But it will come. And when it does, education must be careful lest in reacting against "progressive" education devoid of discipline, they follow the false sacrificial gods, such as the youths of Europe in prostrating before Nazism, Fascism and Communism. The latent capacity for doing the brave and heroic which is in every youth will soon come to the surface, and when it does, please God, it will be both for heroes and saints that they center their affection. The ascetic ideal has passed away from the elders, but God sends fresh generations into the world to give the world a fresh start. Our teen-agers will one day find their right ideals, in love of country and love of God, and particularly the latter, for it is the function of religion to make possible to men sacrifices which in the face of reason or egotism would never come to the surface.

CHAPTER 29

More about Teen-Agers

WHAT AMERICANS call "teen-agers," or adolescents, covers that period midway between springtime and summer. As what happens to the trees and the blossoms during March determines the fruit, so the experiences of teen-agers help mould their maturity. Some youths, like some fruits, ripen too soon, and others never seem to ripen, but there are others who fulfill the best aspirations of an older generation.

The psychology of teen-agers is as important as it is interesting. The three dominant characteristics are: interiority, imitation and restlessness.

Interiority: A trait often missed because of the energy of youth is its consciousness of solitude and its sense of aloofness born of the realization that a kind of barrier is thrown up between itself and the world. Boys try sometimes to overcome this barrier by shaving before their time, thus leaping the wall between adolescence and manhood; girls affect it in dress or other mannerisms in order to bridge the gap. Gestures are clumsy, uneasy, ungraceful; arms seem too long and always in the way; words have little value for exchange purposes with adults in establishing contact with the grown world. There are more images than ideas in the interior world, which may account in part for the inability to establish rapport with others. Sometimes this very ineptitude increases interiority and drives the youth back into himself or herself. Because exterior actions do not always give release to the inner world, the teen-ager often has recourse to an inner world of images where he or she has an interior adventure, picturing himself as a hero on a football field, or herself as married to a prince. Movies are popular because they are a good feeder for such day dreams and hopes. The general picture, however, is of one who has suddenly arrived at a growing interior depth but, not knowing its value, expresses himself or herself badly.

Imitation: There is a profound philosophical reason for imitation. The ego is under the imperative and need of emerging from itself as a chrysalis; the interior is bursting to affirm its personality. Imitation becomes a substitute for originality; originality commits the youth to effort, labor, pain, perseverance and sometimes the scorn of others; but imitation gives one the needed exteriorization through a kind of social conformism. Locked up in itself, youth must emerge. Since it is harder to be oneself, and at that age one does not quite know what is oneself, it becomes a hero-worshipper; hence the fan clubs, fanaticism for players of percussion instruments, the idolizing of some so-called movie star.

That is why in the high school age one finds very few who ever dress outside of the pattern set by a few. The creative minority in adult life is few; therefore the youth must not be taken to task for imitation. This mimicry could be dangerous if what was idolized were low; but it can be also one of the ennobling influences of youth if those who are imitated are noble, good and patriotic. Youth imitates because it wants to create and creation marks the end of interiority in a constructive way.

Restlessness: Perhaps a better description of restlessness would be a mercurial affection. There is extreme mobility in youth, due to the multitude of impressions which flood the soul. Life is multiple; there is little harmony because of the great variety of appeals from the external world. Hence the appeal of certain youths of a certain type of jitterbug music; it provides a muscular outlet for sense energy which has not yet been rationalized. Because of this agitation, it is difficult for a youth to fix his or her attention on any one object; perseverance in study is hard; the impulsions of the moment solicit with a loud voice. This could end in delinquency if the activity never found a target. But at the same time, like the other characteristics, it can also be the salvation of the youth, for he is really running around the circumference of human experience in order to decide on which particular segment he will settle for life; he tours the world of professions, avocations and positions and then decides in which he will repose. Once this energy becomes canalized, focused and rationalized, it becomes the beginning of a life's work and an adolescent begins to be what God intended him to be—a man who in loving virtue knows how to love a woman, a friend and his country.

CHAPTER 30

The Loves of Youth

Every youth is full of incertitude and a latent anxiety. This is because life has not yet been brought to unity. What is immediate and present solicits him with such force that there is little thought of over-all goal and purpose. To cover up this uneasiness, a youth often imagines what a psychologist might call a *Super-self*. It is not another image of himself, but rather the image of something that will complete himself and bring him to unity. This *Super-self* is what we desire to be to complete our personality and what we sometimes fear we never will be. It is almost like the acorn imagining the oak, the bud imagining the flower, and the foundation the roof. It is the completion of all aspirations, the realization of our dream. *"The young men dream dreams, the old men see visions."* The young look ahead, the aged look back. The young, like the rivulet look forward to the sea which will immerse them in joy; the old, like the sea look backwards to the rivulets.

Hence in the love of youths there is a tendency to admire those who complete its incompleteness. Basically, this is nothing else than a love of God Who alone can satisfy all the aspirations of the heart. He, therefore, who believes himself completely satisfied, who never reaches out for a perfection which he has not at this moment, is incapable of loving. Every youth falls in love with the image of the possible, that is, with his dream walking, his emptiness filled, and his yearnings realized. Gustave Thibon once said that *"every woman promises that which only God can give."* By this he meant that the love every heart wants is the infinite; woman seems to give this to man, but actually what man wants is not the lovable but Love which is Divine. In literature, it is not uncommon to find women described as the image of the possible, for example, Beatrice for Dante. No one really knows if Beatrice ever existed. But certainly her influence was greater because she remained as the possible ideal. Everyone carries within himself a blueprint of his ideal. Some day this ideal is seen and though it is called *"love at first sight"* it could conceivably be that which was always loved, but never seen before. Our ideal, or Super-self may even induce us to put ourselves in situations favorable to seeing it realized, as a man who loves dueling seeks out the company of those who duel. Youth seeks out the person who will complete the interior circuit, who will fulfill a desire which is basically for God, but which for a time substitutes for Him. Everyone loves the whole more than the part. Therefore everyone loves God more than His lover reflected in creatures. In most, however, this love is unconscious rather than conscious.

The great mystery of life is really not that we want to be loved, but that we are loved. We need love because we are imperfect; but why anyone should love the imperfect is not easy to understand. That is why all lovers consider themselves unworthy. The beloved is on a pedestal, the lover is on his knees professing his unworthiness. Love always comes as an undeserved gift. To abandon or be unfaithful to that love is to hurt the whole personality, for it destroys the image that was first there. The destruction of the image of the possible is to condemn oneself to a heartache as one feels the truth of the cruel words of Ovid: *"I cannot live either with you or without you."*

This Super-self, or ideal, or image of the possible manifests itself in different ways in a young man and a young woman. In the former, there is a delight found in giving reasons why she is the ideal. Thus does he rationalize his ideal proving to himself and to others that the ideal has come to life. In the latter, however, she strives to intensify the idea that she is the ideal by seeming flight. To attract she appears to fly, thus making her more of an ideal to the pursuer. But in each case the true and absolute ideal is not found. That is God. But it is only later on in life that youth realizes that what he wanted was *"the love we fall just short of in all love"*—the love of the Infinite with *"passionless passion and wild tranquility!"*

MAN'S GOAL

CHAPTER 31

The Master Value

THE FIRST DECISION any traveler makes is to choose his destination. After he knows where he is going, he can then decide what means he will use on the journey—automobile or foot, plane or train. The wise man will proceed by the same ordered method in planning how to live, for life, too, is a journey. It, too, must have a goal, reasonably chosen, before we can decide how best to spend our energies and pass our days.

The man who consciously directs his actions so that he will save his soul has Eternity and God as a goal. This is the conduct normal to man. There are people who, like Macbeth, look on life as a "tale told by an idiot, full of sound and fury, signifying nothing." But they only arrived at this despairing belief, like Macbeth, when their unrepented crimes made them dread the judgment of an after-life. Atheism is the wish fulfillment of those who do not want to believe that anyone, even a Merciful God, is "on to them"; no one denies immortality unless he feels that his own life gives him reason to dread immortality. The cynic did not think his way to his present beliefs; he sinned, and then adopted a slogan to make the sins seem legitimate. He lived first, and later devised a set of beliefs to justify his actions. Rationalizations follow on behavior; they do not precede it.

Many atheists and agnostics attempt to give life some meaning and purpose by choosing a single, temporal master-value and making it their goal. They choose a "destination" and they do only those things that seem to advance them towards it. The self-indulgent thus conduct a lifelong search for pleasure. The proud seek only to make others acknowledge them as gods and goddesses. A man can find his master-value easily: it is the thing the loss of which would make him saddest, the thing which, if finally attained, would make him happiest.

Many people today have taken as their goal the obtainment of wealth. This is an inferior "destination," for it reduces man's dignity, making him serve something lesser than himself—for material goods are inferior to human personality. Other people chase after honors, publicity and fame. These are also unsatisfying and unworthy goals; anyone who steps into a shower, where he cannot carry his press-clippings, knows that his celebrity has not elevated him above other men. To make "what people say" an aim in life is to court a nervous breakdown by becoming the slave of every copywriter's whim.

A true goal in living must take into account the nature of man: what he was made to do, what he longs to have. The faculties which set man apart from the animals are the intellect (which naturally seeks to know all truth) and the will (which longs to embrace all goodness). But we know that Perfect Truth and Perfect Good are to be found only in God; the complete fulfillment of our natures is thus impossible except in Him. And happiness we derive from pursuing God as a master-value, as a goal, is not subject to the accidents of our life on earth; it arises within the soul itself. The man who has God as a goal knows peace such as the world cannot give and cannot destroy.

When God is once chosen as the Master-Value, we have a yardstick by which to measure actions and to know how good or bad they are. A man is "doing good" so long as he is directing his course towards God; he does evil when he turns away from Him. The journey towards God in this life is a preparation for the Light of Glory, the enjoyment of Him in Eternity. To win through to this enduring ecstasy is the proper goal for which all men are born; when we are travelling towards it, we are "good," i. e., we are performing the purpose for which we were made. A pencil is "good" if it writes well; a race horse is "good" if it runs well; a man is "good" if he fulfills well his purpose of knowing, loving, serving God in preparation for Eternity.

Only the God-centered life gives us an adequate way of measuring the worth of this action versus that. The materialist may think he will live pleasantly by making pleasure his goal; but he cannot, for self-centered pleasures pall and lose their tang with repetition. The proud man may imagine that power and prestige will fill his hungry heart; they will not, for such goals make us cruel and treacherous, and leave us in a stately isolation from our kind. Life soon loses zest and meaning to those who have found no goal greater than themselves towards which to regulate their days.

But once the true goal is found in God alone, everything is ordered by the law of love. The dominant passion, now, is to preserve a loving relationship—first with God Himself and then, as a sequence of this, with family, friends, associates and even enemies, for love of God. The world is no longer filled with people and things on whom we have projected our selfish will; it is crowded with creatures who are precious and delectable because each one of them can, somehow, advance us on our journey towards our Goal, Who is our God.

CHAPTER 32

Wealth and Power

In past ages men talked less about "living their lives" and more about saving their souls. They did not lay as much stress as we do on political and economic matters, but they took far more interest in things moral and religious. Now, since the attraction of Heaven has lessened for many men, their attachment to the earth has become intensified. The quest for God has given way to the quest for wealth and power. The idol of our century is not the saint, but the man who has won through to "the top."

Two extreme attitudes confront the modern mind as it revolves the question of how much importance it should attach to the standard of worldly success. Should such a thing be worshipped, sought after as the greatest good in life? Should it, on the other hand, be condemned as vicious in itself? The ambitious men of our century adopt the first extreme attitude. The second is shared by two kinds of revolutionary: the Anarchist, who condemns all power, and the Communist, who censures all wealth.

There is only one sound standard by which such viewpoints can be tested, and that is the life of Our Lord. The incidents narrated in the Gospels show that power and wealth are legitimate ambitions and ideals, but with certain safeguards the modern world usually ignores. These safeguards are revealed to us in the hidden life of Our Lord in Nazareth, and they are two: No man has a right to power until he has learned obedience, as Christ was obedient to His parents. And no man may safely possess wealth until he has learned to be detached from it, as Our Lord was, when He chose for His early vocation that of a poor village carpenter.

Here, then, was a Power Who became weak, a Master Who became as servant, a Lord Who came to minister to others. Submission to His Father was the prelude to every showing-forth of miracles or authority: and so it must be with us. All powers . . . political, industrial, social and economic . . . must become subject to the Power above them and must regulate themselves to God's design before they may rightly claim subservience from anyone. Power is not to be checked from below, by the anarchist's defiance or the revolutionary's *coup*, but it is to find its limitations from above. Earthly powers may properly ask to be obeyed when they are obedient to the Power That stands over them; they may demand respect for their authority when they follow the wishes of their Author; they can ask for reverence when they themselves have stooped to revere their God.

It is much the same with wealth: Our Lord teaches us that no one is entitled to it until he has learned to be detached from it. The Nazareth years are not intended to glorify poverty in our eyes, to teach us a fatalistic resignation to squalid living conditions, or to preach stoical endurance of hardship and hunger for themselves. Our Lord was poor. He worked hard to earn the bare necessities of life. He was a needy carpenter. But He was a Rich God, Who owned the universe, and He was a God of Power Who had made Himself powerless. Wealth and power are not, of themselves, evil, for both of them belong to God.

Thus the Communists, who harangue the rich for *being* rich, find no support in Christianity. No one has the right to despise the rich until, like Our Lord, he has proven himself free from the passion to possess . . . and then he will not wish to despise anyone. The poverty of Nazareth was not a condemnation of wealth nor a glorification of poverty: it was an illustration of the beautiful doctrine of detachment. Christ's followers, too, were able to free themselves from possessions for the greater glory of God, even though their possessions might amount only to a few fishing boats and tangled nets and the greater gift of their free wills.

Our Lord never tried to induce the poor to accept poverty as a good, or misery as a thing to be sought for itself. He glorified neither the poor man nor the rich man. But the one He did praise was the poor man who, having once been rich, had willingly made himself poor . . . the poor man who, by detaching himself from everything, became possessed of everything—the man who, wanting nothing, owned all things. For Our Lord does not canonize the "giving up" of wealth in favor of a vacuum; He approves, rather, of giving wealth in exchange for the far greater riches of Heaven. He did not tell us "Blessed are the poor," or "Blessed are the rich." But He told us, "Blessed are the poor in spirit."

The Hidden Life of Nazareth does not preach a mere truism about the "beauty of poverty" or the "holiness of weakness": these things are not, in themselves, Christian virtues. The Nazareth lesson is a far richer paradox, teaching us the richness of those who, through detachment, become the poor in spirit, and the power of those who make themselves weak to serve. Our Blessed Lord is thus the only One Who ever walked the earth of whom Rich and Poor, Masters and Servants, Powerful and Weak may all claim for their own, and say truthfully of Him, "He came from our ranks, and He is One of ours."

CHAPTER 33

God Is Self-Preserving

I F OUR WILLS are on the side of God, we cannot be discouraged, for the side which we have chosen is always victorious, is never flouted. God is self-preserving, and evil is self-defeating. The reality of things is ever on the side of God.

Evil is necessarily unstable, because it runs counter to the nature of things as they were made. All the laws of our human nature nudge us toward our proper destiny of holiness, as of health. If we attend to our bodies properly, obeying the rules of health, we are healthy; if we break these laws, our rebellion brings sickness . . . and few of us would take proper care of ourselves if the violation of the laws of health did *not* carry some penality, as a reminder.

We are free in this and other fields to break the laws God has set down, but we are not free to escape the penalty that breaking His laws entails. To jump from a window does not destroy the law of gravitation; but it may destroy our lives. Nature is on God's side, always; it will betray our wants, but never His commands. And this is as true in the moral sphere as in the physical.

When men sin, there is no need for God to intervene to see that they are punished: our natures are so made that we cannot oppose Him without being in opposition to ourselves. If we break the law of temperance, a headache follows. God did not send that headache by a special Act; He had already made us in such a way that our evil deeds result in evil effects. The poet Francis Thompson describes how even things turn against us when we do not use them for God's purposes. He calls created objects "servitors":

"I tempted all His servitors, but to find
My own betrayal in their constancy
In faith to Him, in fickleness to me,
Their traitorous trueness, and their loyal deceit."

When Peter denied our Lord, the cock crowed, causing him great pain. The very barnyard had turned on Peter, for Nature belongs to God.

When we reject the moral law, we suffer . . . not because we *intended* evil, but simply because we defied a force stronger than ourselves: the reality of things. In sinning, we thus produce an effect which we did not intend; this never happens as a result of our good actions. If I use a pencil to write with, the pencil is un-harmed; if I try to open a tin can with it, I break it in two. I have used the pencil in a way contrary to its purpose, and so destroyed it.

If I live my life according to its highest purpose . . . and that is the attainment of Truth and Love . . . I will perfect it. If I live according to my animal impulses, I frustrate myself as surely as I would frustrate a razor by using it to hew a stone.

Evil is always mutilation of the self. If I live as I ought to live, I become a man; if I live as my whims dictate, I become a beast, and an unhappy beast. This is not a result I ever planned, but it is still unavoidable. The man who wills to over-drink does not intend to ruin his health, but he does just that. The man who overeats does not count on indigestion, but he gets it. The man who wills to steal has not aimed at prison, yet that is where he lands.

When a traveller refuses to follow the guide-posts showing him the right way, he may still, eventually, reach his goal by finding disappointment at the end of every false trail. Disorder is a stern teacher, and a slow one, but a certain one. The Spanish have a proverb: *"He who spits against Heaven spits in his own face."* Evil may triumph for a little while. It can win the first battle, but it loses the booty and the reward.

Caesar built roads to carry the screaming eagles of Rome across the world in military triumph; but over those roads Peter and Paul carried the Gospels, instead. Thus the end of this very century will see scientists and philosophers picking out of the wastebasket of the universities all the Sacred and Divine Truths which the Eighteenth and Nineteenth Centuries threw away.

For good is self-preserving. Evil defeats itself.

INNER PEACE

CHAPTER 34

"Getting Away with It"

BEHIND EVERY ATTEMPT to "get away with it" is the belief that one will never be found out. If there is only one check on the books, one can be reasonably secure that there will be no discovery of the theft, but if there is a second check by a master bookkeeper, one is less inclined to commit the crime. Nothing so much conduces to evil as the belief that this world is all, and that beyond there is not a further judgment on the way we have lived and thought. If this world is all, then why not get all you can out of it and at any cost, providing you can "get away with it."

Contrary to this philosophy is that of Our Lord which said: "What is veiled will all be revealed, what is hidden will all be known." (Luke 12:2) Everything tends from darkness to the light where it may stand in its true judgment. Seeds that are buried seek to pierce their grave; trees in a thick forest bend to more readily absorb the light; shells deep in the sea grope their way to the shore. So the lives of men, however deeply they bury their crimes, will one day push themselves to the Light of Judgment where "each man will be judged according to his works."

Modern psychology is based on the assumption that even in this world man really "gets away" with nothing. His secret hates, his hidden sins, his flippant treading upon the laws of morality —all of these leave their traces in his mind, his heart and his unconsciousness. Like the boy in the ancient fable who concealed in his blouse a fox which he had stolen. While denying his guilt, the fox ate away his entrails. The thousands of people stretched out on psychoanalytical couches may deny morality and guilt, but even while making their denial a real psychologist can see their mind being eaten away. There is nothing hidden that will not be revealed.

Inside of every heart are passions and wishes, hopes and fears, hatreds and lusts, evil intents and hidden guilts; one day all of these shadowy dwellers of the mental underworld will work their way up either to a confession of guilt or else to mental and physical signs of the denial of that guilt. Anyone is free to deny morality, but he is not free to escape the effects of its violation. Sin is written on faces, in the brain, it is seen in the shifting eyes and the hidden fears of night.

If a man knows that his thefts will one day be discovered, he will take every possible means to make recompense before discovery. If a man knows that one day everything he did will not only be revealed to God but also to fellowman, he will purge himself of them, that what was before a debit may now be a credit. To such a soul there is nothing more foolish than trying to "get away with it."

Psychiatry is not as much a modern discovery as it is a modern need. Its method has been known for centuries, but there was never the occasion to apply it, because in other ages men knew they could not "get away with it." Their purgations, reparations and amendments were settled on their knees in prayer, rather than on their back on a couch. But at that moment when the Divine and morality were denied, society came face to face with handling the mental effects which that very denial entailed. The crimes were not new, for people could snap their fingers just as much against the moral law in the days of faith as now. In those days when they did wrong, they knew it was wrong. They lost the road, but they never threw away the map. But today when men do wrong they call it right. This creates in addition to the moral problem which is denied, a *mental* problem. And that is where much psychiatry comes in. There is nothing new about the discovery that the reality we refuse to face we bury in our unconscious mind. What is new is the *need* to treat those who break the law and deny the law; who live by freedom and refuse to accept its consequences. Every soul that violates a law of God sooner or later turns states-evidence against himself. The long tongue of wrong doing will not be quiet. Deny though he may the Divine Judge, his anxieties and fears reveal that there is already a judge seated in his own conscience, condemning even when society approves, and reproving when he himself would deny. There is no secrecy for wickedness. The fear of God may have vanished from modern civilization, but the fear of man has taken its place and therefore made us unhappy. To fear God is to dread hurting one we love, like a child before a devoted father. To fear man is to shrink from threats and cruelty. One day a Great Book will be opened and there even every idle word we uttered will be recorded. Whatever is spoken in darkness will be brought to light, for in the final analysis no man "gets away" with anything.

CHAPTER 35

Inscape

A NEW WORD is needed in our language, and though perhaps it has already been used in the poetry of Gerald Manly Hopkins, it has nevertheless not yet received universal use. This new word ought to be the opposite of *escape*. Escape means to fly from something dangerous in the hope of finding security. It is derived from two Latin words: *ex* "from" and *cappa* "cloak." It means, therefore, to get out of an enclosure, to become free.

But to be free from "a cape" is not to be free really. A man wants to be free "from" something in order to be free "for" something; otherwise, freedom is meaningless. Our modern world is too interested in negative freedom or escape from limitations, and not sufficiently interested in positive freedom or the achievement of Divinely assigned destinies. A rich man went up to a taxi driver and said: "Are you free?" The taxi driver said: "Yes." The rich man left, shouting: "Hurrah for freedom." The taxi driver came to understand for the first time in his life that freedom from limitation becomes meaningful only when there is a definite goal or object to be attained.

The word "escape" has become more familiar today as "escapism." Escapism is flight, an *ersatz* and a substitute for not fulfilling a duty, or fulfilling an obligation. For example, alcoholism is an escape for the man who has piled up debts and tries to forget them in the irresponsibility of sleep. Sleeping tablets are a means of escape to souls whose conscience beats up a rat-a-tat on their brain all through the long and fearful night. Those who are not courageous enough to give up evil habits often try to solace their wickedness by calling those who love God "escapists."

Escapism is cowardice. There can be no peace for the soul until there is an "inscape." An "inscape" means a spiritual, moral and mental security found through being enfolded in the meaning and goal of life.

Tennyson once wrote that if he knew the flower in the crannied wall, root and stem and all, he would know what God and man is. By this he meant that the flower in the crannied wall was the "inscape" of the whole universe. Somehow or other, if one knew it thoroughly, one would see it reflecting the countless generations of flowers that preceded it, all the rain that ever fell from the heavens, all the beams of the sun that shone upon it, all the chemicals of the earth that once hemorrhaged from primitive volcanoes, and above all the Mind of God that made all these things converge in this one flower in the crannied wall. Not only that little flower, but every little thing in the universe, whether it be the filigree of a snowflake with its chiseled patterns, or the birds that sing their Matins to the trees earlier than the monks in their cells—all these things reveal the Creator's Mind. They are a concretion of the Divine Architect's plans.

What then is inscape? It is law, order, rhythm, pattern, purpose. It is a philosophy of life; it is the revelation not only of where I came from, but also of where I am going. Inscape is the discovery of order and meaning; it means being wrapped in the cloak of the mystery of God; the making oneself intelligible and giving life a meaning; it is finding a refuge in the God of love. For every escapism there must be inscapism; for every flight from reality, there must be a return to it; for every loss of personality, there must be its recovery.

Here is where a certain erotic type of psychoanalysis (which is not identical with psychiatry) breaks down. It can tear up and discover the disease, but it cannot heal; it can diagnose, but not cure; it can psychoanalyze, but not psychosynthesize; it can tell a man he has anxiety neuroses, which really means nothing; but it cannot tell him why there is a fundamental anxiety at the basis of life; namely because the cups from which he drinks cannot contain the love for which he yearns. Love of sex is an escape; love of goodness is an inscape. Divorce is an escape; fidelity through trial is inscape. Egotism is an escape; charity is inscape. Because the pleasures of life disgust without satisfying, we see an escape from the let-down feeling. Because the pleasures of union with God satisfy, without disgusting, we seek the beatiful inscape, into His Truth and Love, until finally death is swallowed up in Life. Hell is escape; Heaven is inscape.

CHAPTER 36

The Spirit of Forgiveness

THE ALARMING amount of hatred loose in the modern world is largely caused by guilt: the man who hates himself soon begins to hate his fellowmen. Unconfessed, and sometimes unadmitted sins create a deep unease within the personality . . . the balance has to be, somehow, restored; the self must somehow be placed in a more favorable light. The right way to do this is to admit, confess and do penance for our sins. The wrong way . . . which many unhappy people take today . . . is to make the self seem better, sins and all, by detracting from someone else. The individual who has injured someone he loves often discovers that the act has turned his love to hate: he can now appear innocent in his own eyes only if he accuses the other of grave faults to justify the injury done him. To pass thus from love to hatred is all too easy; but to turn hatred into love is hard, for it can be done only if the self-deception is punctured, the injury confessed.

A second cause of hatred is fear: men who have ceased to fear the Lord soon begin to fear one another. Feeling themselves weak . . . as they are . . . men tremble before the dangers of a "hostile world" they cannot placate or conquer. Fear of God is a very different thing: it is not a servile fear, such as a slave feels toward his tyrant, but a reverential fear, such as a child may have for a loving father. The proper fear of God relieves us from all temporal fears: we trust Him to protect us and to befriend us through all dangers. But those who lack this belief in God direct their fears towards other men and grow to hate their neighbors as so many threats to their security.

Hatred is a dangerous emotion to encourage. It can even become a physical poison: an English medical journal reported the case of a mother whose hatred of her husband affected her milk and poisoned the baby she was nursing. Anger and hatred can also affect the digestive processes, causing dyspepsia and ulcers.

Hatred is hard to stop, for, if let alone, it sets off a chain-reaction. One man's animosity arouses anger in another, who, in turn, creates rage in someone else. That is why Our Lord told us when we are struck on one cheek, to turn the other: thus, by an interior effort of the will, we bring the chain of anger to an end. The only way to destroy hate is for an individual to absorb it and, in his own heart, convert it into love.

Such a course is difficult for us: we men have so small a reservoir of love within us that, if we draw on it, it soon runs dry. We have then to find another source of love in order to forgive . . . a new and added quota of potential mercy.

There are two considerations which make it easier for us to ask God to help us to forgive others. We can remember how many faults of our own He has forgiven us. And we can try to help God in His own perpetual efforts to save the erring soul.

The first consideration is a matter of plain fact: each of us has done worse things to God than any neighbor has ever done to us. That is why Our Lord warns against seeing the speck in our neighbor's eyes and ignoring the great beam in our own: when we recall the offenses we have had forgiven us, then we realize that we are in no position to withhold forgiveness from a neighbor. As our Divine Lord has told us, "I remitted all that debt of thine at thy entreaty; was it not thy duty to have mercy on thy fellowman, as I have mercy on thee?"

The second consideration moving us towards forgiveness can be reduced to earthly terms: suppose that some enemy has done us a very serious injury. But suppose that the father of our enemy comes to us and says that, for years, he has tried to make his son kind and good, but without success. Yet he has not abandoned hope, and he pleads with us that we, too, shall join his efforts to save the son. Such an appeal would soften our hearts.

God is, in fact, such a father. He, Who is long-suffering with

His rebellious children, wishes us to be patient with them, too—to try to help Him bring them to an area of love. This point is brought out in the story told of Abraham in the desert: one night a stranger is said to have approached his tent and implored his hospitality. Abraham gave him the best of food, surrendered his own bed, waited on him . . . but the stranger complained and up-braided and found fault. Abraham was about to turn him out, in anger at his ingratitude, when God spoke to him: "Abraham," he said, "I have put up with that man for forty years. Can't you stand him for one night?"

The ability to forgive others their offenses comes to us only from God, but He will not withhold the power if we ask for it. His own words tell us, "Be merciful then as your Heavenly Father is merciful. Judge nobody, and you will not be judged; condemn nobody, and you will not be condemned; forgive, and you will be forgiven. The measure you award to others is the measure that will be awarded to you."

CHAPTER 37

Inner Life

THE MORE we look for happiness in the outer world, the more we endanger our inner peace. Only the man who is self-possessed is serene, for he alone has set up conditions for peace which are under his own control. The others are victims of circumstance, slaves of things which any moment may withhold. The drunkard is alcohol-possessed; the avaricious are money-possessed; the trifling are style-possessed . . . the universe of any one of them can be rocked by somebody else's will. None of us can control the way in which others will act toward us; but we can always control our reaction to them.

Our relations with external things are all in terms of having or of not having; the inner life of the spirit centers, in contrast, on being, on what one is. Too often people spoil their whole lives in desires to *have,* when our main interests should be devoted to efforts to *be.* Since nothing in the material universe is greater than the spirit, the personality within each of us, every yielding of ourselves to some material craving or necessity is a loss. Having anything at all creates problems; the more keys a man carries on his key-ring, the more numerous his problems. And not-having things we think we need can cause frustration, too. But the man who wants nothing is free; whatever happens to him is acceptable, and whatever is withheld from him is surrendered without a pang.

Refusal to value the external things as a goal is the pathway to self-possession. To be wholly integrated and happily simple, as we ought to be, demands that we flee from the chaotic, the multitudinous and conflicting objects that surround us. For if we allow these things to fill our souls, they will crowd out the Divine which ought to dwell there. The man who relies on outside satisfactions is in a constant state of civil war; he is the house divided against itself which cannot stand.

In this age many things solicit us to look for happiness among cheap and material satisfactions which require no inner effort, no use of the reason or the will. Even our magazines now tend more and more to use pictures instead of text: we do not even have to read or think to "keep up". Stimuli from stage and screen and billboards pull us in different directions, arouse in us a constant series of emotions, keep us living in a turmoil of surface experiences. This kind of living can make us the victims of our own sensations, which are cruel tyrants; men who surrender inner mastery are heading for a nervous breakdown.

To restore peace to the shattered, nervous man of today, all that is needed is for him to place a ring of silence between himself and the outer world . . . to begin to place more importance on what he *is* than on what he *has* or what he *feels*. If we detach our attention from the ego and its selfish needs, we have made a start. The next step is to try to fulfill, down to the least detail, the Holy Will of God—for doing this affords our self-perfection and our peace. Clinical health and moral health are usually identical. A violation of the moral law always disturbs mind and body, but submission to God's will inevitably brings a greater health to the body and a deep peace to the soul.

For a while, the sacrifice of our selfish whims will demand an effort; but to the man who has once placed God's wishes ahead of his own, there is no further sacrifice involved. The early stages of the spiritual life are like the years of a musician's apprenticeship: he has to think in terms of effortful study, or finger-exercises and of missing parties in order to practice. But later, these things are willingly accepted, for the mature musician sees them as curtain raisers to his joy. The man who loves God with his whole mind and his whole heart sees all obedience to Him as a way to beauty and wonder. As lightning strikes the metal pole which is already full of electricity rather than the wooden shaft, so God's serenity strikes those creatures who are already best prepared for it through love of Him.

Such inner peace can be won only by making God the ruler of *all* that we do. Many people who believe in God refuse to go this far: they keep Him in a small compartment of their minds. Their plans are laid without consulting Him; their trials and sufferings are endured with no recollection of the fact that Love may hurt in order to cure; their days are passed in loneliness and weariness, although each hour might have been filled with sweetness.

To such hearts a single moment of grace may work the change. They suddenly become aware that "the Lord is in the house." Better still: the Lord is in our hearts. They are no longer self-centered, now, but they are God-centered; outer events of their lives can no longer ruffle their peace. What they have has become unimportant; the only thing that matters is what they are, and what they are is His Children. At last they are able to hear His words: "Peace is my bequest to you, and the peace I give you is mine to give; I do not give peace as the world gives it. Do not let your heart be distressed."

CHAPTER 38

A Quick Psychoanalysis

Psychoanalysis originally meant examination of the soul; *this* kind of psychoanalysis, conducted by the individual himself, is valuable. From examining his own soul, any one of us can learn five general truths about all human beings:

1. All of us are dual; we are conscious of a tension between our lofty ideals and their feeble realization—of conflict between what we ought to do and the way we act—of a struggle between our ego, with its longing for supremacy, and the curbs placed on our will by other egos with contradictory desires. There are conflicts between our desire to be free of every restraint, and the slavery to evil habits we suffer if we *do* throw off restraint; between the longing to be ourselves, and the fact that our best pleasures constantly take us out of ourselves. This state of tension is an endemic state in man.

2. Such a conflict is confined to man: animals know no such agonies of indecision between two apparent goods, pulling them in different directions at the same time. This difference gives us a clue to the cause of all our tensions: for man has an immortal soul, and animals have not. We men are plagued with conflicts because we are suspended between the finite and the infinite; we are like mountain climbers halfway up, who aspire to the peak above, and shudder for fear of falling into the abyss below us.

3. Since we are all a composite of body and soul, each of us must make a choice between the two directions in which he can move: he can rise above himself or descend below his present state. He can surmount his human level by seeking God with all the passionate ardor of his soul; or he can slip down to the despair, frustration, melancholy of those who have ceased to seek goodness. For the boundaries of humanity can be crossed in either of two directions: upwards through faith, or downwards to insanity. Every man at every hour moves towards one condition or the other; he cannot remain normal on the merely human level, for our own egos are too narrow and squalid to serve as fitting dwellings for our immortal souls.

The men and women who, neglecting every effort to improve their souls, assert that they are happy anyway are merely lying to us and to themselves: their despair may be invisible, as yet, but it is latent and it is real. Let a crisis come upon such people, and the distress they concealed is evident enough. Suicides among those who lose their money or who are crossed in love reveal that only a thin, illusory substitute for the love of life saved them, until now, from their deep despair of the goodness of the universe.

4. But if the only alternative for us is between pursuit of the infinite God for whom we were made and the agony of despair, why does anyone ever turn his back upon the Eternal?

There are two barriers separating men from a happy destiny, and either one of them may cause a timid man or woman to hold back and sink into despair. Some men are unwilling to make the intellectual effort to seek truth for its own sake, to try to discover what this life is "all about," to humble their pride sufficiently to admit that God may be other than their present conception of Him, and that, to reach Him, they may still have many new things to learn and believe. That refusal holds back the proud from happiness. But there is another obstacle to belief: the refusal to admit Divinity because of the demands such a belief would make on us, and because we dare not face life without the habits of lust and avarice and selfishness which Faith would ask us to surrender.

5. The man who truly "enters into himself" is never pleased at what he finds there: the inner emptiness can drive him to despair. But there are two kinds of emptiness . . . the vast vacuum of a canyon which will never be filled and the expectant emptiness of a nest, hollowed out in preparation for the birth of the birds. So

there are two kinds of despair: the Satanic despair, which refuses to give in to God's mercy, and the creative despair of those who allow their misery to be remedied by God. The first way of despairing was that of Judas, who went out and hanged himself. The second way was that of David, who cried, *"Have mercy on me, O God; have mercy on me."*

So long as such mercy is available for all who despair of their own confusion and conflicts and inner incompleteness, it follows that sin is never the worst thing that can happen to a man. The worst thing is the refusal to recognize his sins. For if we are sinners, there is a Saviour. If there is a Saviour, there is a Cross. If there is a Cross, there is a way of appropriating it to our lives, and our lives to it. When that is done, despair is driven out and we have the *"peace which the world cannot give."*

CHAPTER 39

Self-Discipline

THE PHILOSOPHY of self-expression is so much taken for granted today that few there are who analyze its meaning. Self-expression is right when it means acting according to reason and our higher nature; it is wrong when it means acting in accordance with our instincts and lower nature. A hunter is self-expressive in the right way when he hunts animals in season; he is wrong when he goes hunting mothers-in-law, in season or out of season. Those who identify self-expression with license, or the right to do whatever they please, think that self-discipline is self-destruction, but actually it is only taming the lower for the sake of the higher. The violinist does not break the string when he tunes it to concert-pitch; the sculptor does not destroy the marble when he chisels it to produce the image.

When the chastening of self comes from the outside, it is affiliation; when it comes from the inside by an act of our own will, it is self-discipline. In either case, its purpose is the emergence of a truer and better character. God never permits an affliction except for the purposes of purification. Scripture goes so far as to say that "Whom the Lord loveth tenderly He chasteneth." A young man who loves a young woman wants to see her dressed in a most becoming manner; she, too, suits the color of her dress and the fashion of her hair to his taste. All egotistic wishes are expunged for the sake of the beloved. God, too, sometimes shakes all the leaves off the trees which surround our self-existence in order that we may see the heavens.

Sometimes even the death of a child is God's way of making

parents look beyond this world to the next. When a shepherd finds that his sheep have exhausted the lower pastures, but refuse to climb to greener pastures, he will take a young lamb in his arms to the heights of the mountain side, and the other sheep will follow. The mother eagle gets her young to fly by pecking away pieces of the nest bit by bit, until finally the young have to leave the temporary security. God, too, sometimes has to disturb man in his economic security, lest he think that it is the only security there is.

But over and above the passive discipline from without, there is the active discipline. There is no evil propensity of the heart that is so powerful that it cannot be subdued by discipline. Every man is like an onion. His superficial self has many layers of skins, and at the center of them all is his real self. Self-abnegation tears off all the outer deceptions and finally reveals our true character. One of the reasons why so few know God is because they do not know themselves. They live in a world of make-believe where nothing is real, and thus miss the Ground of all Reality.

We of the Western World have begun to falsely believe that a character is made by external works, and that it matters little what a man does or thinks or wills on the inside. But this can be an escape, for a man can plunge into work to try to forget himself, just as a man can plunge into alcohol to forget himself. When anything goes wrong, the undisciplined blames things—as the golfer blames the clubs for the poor shot, or the clumsy carpenter the tools for inferior work. Actually the fault lies within the disordered and selfish self.

If a man gives up his wealth, his time, and his energy to others, but actually does not give up himself, he has given up nothing. But he who has had some wealth and some honor, but has denied himself, then he is most free. When Our Blessed Lord said that a man must hate himself, He did not mean those qualities in him which make for God-likeness, but rather those barnacles of selfishness which prevent him from becoming all that love has destined for him. There has been no greater secret of inner peace ever given than in the words of John the Baptist when he saw Our Lord coming: "He must increase; I must decrease."

CHAPTER 40

Kindness

MANY PEOPLE who are very kind in their own homes and offices can become very unkind and selfish once they get behind the steering wheel of an automobile. This is probably due to the fact that in their own home they are known; in the automobile they have the advantage of anonymity and hence can be almost brutal without the fear of discovery. To be kind out of fear of others thinking we are unkind is not real kindness, but rather a disguised form of egotism.

The word "kindness" is derived from kindred or kin, and therefore implies an affection which we bear naturally to those who are our flesh and blood. The original and archetypal kindness is that of a parent for a child and a child for a parent, an idea which is preserved in the German language where *Kind* means child. Gradually the word gained in extension until it embraced everyone whom we are to treat as a relative. Unkindness is therefore unnaturalness.

Because kindness is related to love, it follows that the kind person loves another not for the pleasure the other person gives, nor because the other person can do us a kindness in return, but because the other person is lovable in himself. The basic reason why everyone is lovable is because God made him. If we were evolved from the beast, none of us would be deserving of any love.

Since God finds us lovable because He put some of His love into us so we can find others lovable, because we put some of our love into them. But to do this implies a basic kindness which is always prepared to be pleasant with other people. If we start with the belief that most people in the world are crooks, it is amazing how many crooks we find. If, however, we go into the world with the assumption that every one is nice, we are constantly running into nice people. To a great extent the world is what we make it. We get back what we give. If we sow hate, we reap hate; if we scatter love and gentleness we harvest love and happiness. Other people are like a mirror which reflects back on us the kind of image we cast. The kind man bears with the infirmities of others, never magnifies trifles and avoids a spirit of fault finding. He knows that the trouble with most people in the world is that they are unloved. No one cares for them either because they are ugly or nasty, or troublesome, or so-called bores. To a great extent their character is made by the resentment they feel to others who are unkind. One of life's greatest joys comes from loving those whom no one else loves. Thus do we imitate Our Heavenly Father Who certainly cannot see much in any of us creatures that is very attractive. It is curious that most people are more kind to the blind than they are to the deaf. Aristotle commented upon this fact, saying that sight is the most spiritual of all the senses and hearing the most material. For that reason we are moved by sympathy towards those who are afflicted in the most spiritual way. This psychological explanation, however, in no way justifies a want of kindness to either.

Kindness towards the afflicted becomes compassion, which means a suffering with, or an entering into the distress and the pains of others as if they were our own. It enlarges the interest of the heart beyond all personal interest and prompts us to give either what we have in the form of alms, or the giving of one's talent as a doctor may treat a poor patient, or the giving of one's time which is sometimes the hardest thing of all to give. The truly compassionate and kind man who gives up his time for others manages to find time. Like the bread, miraculously multiplied, he gives, and yet he gathers up for himself more than he gave.

Many psychiatrists today know very well that all they have to do to help certain distressed minds is to listen to their stories.

Convince the anxious heart that you know the secret of his anxiety and he is already half cured. Even if we can convince the enemy that we have no bitterness in our heart against him, his arm will fall helpless at his side. All mental abnormalities have their roots in selfishness, all happiness has its roots in kindness. But to be really kind, one must see in everyone an immortal soul to be loved for God's sake. Then everyone is precious.

CHAPTER 41

Fear and Ethics

MOST NEUROSES are bulwarks against fear. Many psychologists and physicians have come to adopt this thesis inasmuch as fear does provoke some kind of self defense. It is actually not fear that is feared; the enemy is the tension between the conscience and what has happened. Fear is like the gauge on a steam boiler. It merely registers pressure.

The simplest way but the worst way to remove fear from the conscious mind is to repress it—that is, to relegate it into unconsciousness. When unexpected visitors come to the house, a housewife will take old linen and dirty shirts which lie about the front room and toss them into the cellar. The mind does the same thing; it defends itself against tormenting sensations by throwing them into the unconsciousness.

The effects of suppressing fear are manifold. First on the physical side they may be palpitation, migraine, cramps, convulsions, etc. On the mental side the repressed fear comes out as anger, depression and surliness. One psychologist tells the story of a small boy who wept copiously whenever he heard bells tolled for a funeral. He had often wished that his parents were dead, but he repressed the wish. He had fear as a result of the wish and he escaped it by weeping. His fear resulted from the guilt of wishing his parents dead and he sublimated it by tears.

Lady Macbeth had induced her ambitious husband to murder the King, their guest, while he slept, and then to assume the crown. When her husband is shaken by the act she reminds him:

> *"These deeds must not be thought*
> *After these ways, so it will make us mad."*

This is an excellent description of the pathological effects of the murderer's endeavor to escape fear. She is trying to drown conscience by saying that one must not think of the deed in terms of right and wrong. Yet all the while that she is repressing it she is inducing her own madness. She tells her husband to wash his hands and then to smear the grooms with blood. Since he is afraid to do so, she kills the grooms herself and then smears their bodies with the blood. Then she exclaims:

> *"My hands are your color, but I shame*
> *To wear a heart so white. . . .*
> *A little water clears us of this deed."*

Here she tries to convince herself and her husband again that one must not seek to have a clean heart; that there is no judge within the human breast, and that all one hast to do is to clear oneself of the external consequences.

Conscience still produces its effects; she who tried to deny it now has a compulsion neurosis which expresses itself in the constant washing of hands:

> *"Who would have thought the old man*
> *To have so much blood in him. . . .*
> *Will these hands ne'er be clean?"*

First she thought that the guilt of the murder could be cleansed by washing away the blood; now she has to wash away the fear of guilt, as she admits with her husband that all the waters of the seven seas are not enough to wash the blood from her hands.

There are some people who wash their hands after touching door knobs and who repeat this process as many as ten times before they get out of the house. This signifies a need of cleansing and it is thought that the external washings will be a substitute for the moral and inner washing which is denied because of repressed guilt. This does not mean to say that all those who suffer from guilt have violated some moral principle; but it does mean that those who have done so can never expect to have their fears lifted by mere treatment of the external symptoms.

Medical treatment in dealing with fear should never neglect the moral principles which may possibly be behind fear and their manifestations in body and mind. Even Freud has admitted that from a medical point of view the unscrupulous method of satisfying every instinct may make the patient worse. Ethics is the very essence of sound medical treatment.

CHAPTER 42

Rest and Meditation

MODERN MAN would be far happier if he would take a little time off to meditate. As the Old Testament prophet said: "Peace, peace and there is no peace, but no man considereth in his heart." The Gospel tells us that Our Blessed Lord withdrew Himself from the crowds into the wilderness and prayed. Martha, who was too busy about many things, was told that only one thing was necessary. A life of faith and with peace of soul can be cultivated only by periodical isolation from the cares of the world.

There are various kinds of weariness: weariness of the body, which can be satisfied under any tree or even on a pillow of stone; weariness of the brain, which needs the incubation of rest for new thought to be born; but hardest of all to satisfy is weariness of heart, which can be healed only by communion with God.

Silence helps speech; retirement helps thinking. A contemporary of Abraham Lincoln tells us that he spent three weeks with Lincoln just after the Battle of Bull Run: "I could not sleep. I was repeating the part that I was to play in a public performance. The hour was past midnight. Indeed, it was coming near to dawn, when I heard low tones coming from the room where the President slept. The door was partly open. I instinctively walked in and there I saw a sight which I shall never forget. It was the President, kneeling beside an open Bible. The light was turned low in the room. His back was turned toward me. For a moment I was silent, as I stood looking in amazement and wonder. Then he cried out in tones so pleading and sorrowful: 'O thou God that heard Solomon in the night that he prayed for wisdom, hear me; I cannot lead this people, I cannot guide the affairs of this nation without Thy help. I am poor and weak and sinful. O God, who didst hear Solomon when he cried to Thee, hear me and save this nation'."

One wonders how many of our public officials in the great burdens that are laid upon them ever cry to God for help. When the United Nations held its first meeting in San Francisco, fearful that we might offend the atheists, it was decided to keep a minute of silence instead of praying fearlessly to God to illumine and guide the nations. It was in the moment of Peter's failure in fishing that Our Lord said: "Launch out into the deep." It is in the times of our failures that the soul must draw away from the shores.

What the Saviour promises in the retirement is "rest for your souls." Rest is a gift; it is not earned; it is not the payment for finishing a job; it is the dowry of grace. Greed, envy, wealth and avarice think of rest in terms of the good things of the world; true rest is the stilling of passions, the control of wavering ambitions, the joy of a quiet conscience. There is no rest until life has been made intelligible. Most of the restlessness of souls today comes from not knowing why they are here, or where they are going, and they refuse to take time out to solve that problem. Until it is solved, nothing is solved. There is not even much sense in going on living unless one knows why he is living.

Driving power is always associated with inner repose; otherwise energy is explosiveness and imprudent action. They that *wait* upon the Lord shall *renew* their strength. The renewals of strength are less physical than they are spiritual. A tired soul makes a tired body more often than a tired body makes a tired soul. The rest which Christianity enjoins is less cessation from work than it is freedom from the anxieties that come from guilt and avarice. Spiritual refreshment in prayer, retreat, meditation are the most potent influences for restoring harmony to the thousands of nervous patients. Life, like music, must have its rhythm of silence as well as sound.

The rest which retirement and contemplation give is not just a rest from toil, but it is even a rest in toil. The peace of Christ is not a hothouse plant; it raises its head for the storms; it is peace for the battle and joy of conscience for those who assail conscience. The world cannot give it; the world cannot take it away. It is not given by outward circumstance; it rules in the heart; it is an inward state. To be spiritually minded is to have rest.

GIVING

CHAPTER 43

Better to Give Than Receive

THE VAST MAJORITY of the people in Western civilization are engaged in the task of getting. Strange as it may seem, the Christian ethic is founded on the opposite principle, that it is more blessed to give than to receive. Both the opportunity and the burden of filling this Divine mandate falls principally upon those of us who live in a civilization that has been abundantly blessed by God. The per capita income of the United States is about $1,500 a year, and yet the per capita income of one third of the world's population is less than $50 a year, while two thirds of the world's population is living on less than $200 a year. In the United States $28 out of every $100 is paid into the government as taxes. We pay more in taxes than most people of the world earn to keep body and soul together.

We are, of course, a nation helping the socially disinherited people of the world; we have even given an example of loving our enemies in war by helping their economic restoration. But here our concern is less with the national spirit of giving, than it is with the personal spirit. The reason it is more blessed to give than to receive is because it helps to detach the soul from the material and the temporal in order to ally it with a spirit of altruism and charity which is the essence of religion. Cicero once said that "men resemble gods in nothing so much as in doing good to their fellow creatures." Aristotle says that by narrowness and selfishness, by envy and ill will, men degenerate into beasts and become wolves and tigers to one another; but by goodness and love, by mutual compassion and helpfulness, men become gods to one another.

The history of the Jews reveals how much their temporal blessing was consecrated to the service of God and to aiding the poor. In the best days of their history, their tithes and offerings, their thank-offerings and their free will offerings, were on a scale of splendid munificence; nor did they lose thereby for they were constantly thanking God for their many blessings. Even today that same spirit of generosity has characterized these people, not only to their own brethren, but also to Protestants and to Catholics.

On a smaller scale, it will be found that the unity of a community depends to a great extent upon the services and kindnesses of one individual to another. The farming population of any country in the world is a perfect example of this altruism. At harvest time, each farmer helps every other farmer, and when there is a death in the family, willing hands are always found to pick the corn and cut the wheat.

There is not always the same spirit in the large cities, partly due to the anonymity of the masses, and partly due to competition. Where most people we meet are strangers, there is a tendency to lock one's self in his shell. One notices this particularly in driving an automobile. Men who are very gentle at home and kind to friends, become like raging beasts growling at the stupidity of every other driver once they get behind a wheel where anonymity protects them.

Giving is really a divinely appointed way of acknowledging the mercies of God. We have indeed nothing to offer anyway that we have not received, and yet He is pleased to accept our offerings as tokens of our gratitude. Egotism makes the self the center; altruism and charity make the neighbor the center. Only on the principle of giving can the inequalities of the human race be adjusted, can the strong help the weak, and social peace reign among men. Many a man when he was poor had a heart that was open to every call of pity, but as riches increased he set his heart more upon them. The massing of wealth has a peculiar effect on the soul; it intensifies the desire of getting. What is often lust in youth is avarice in old age. Could they but expose themselves to the great joy of giving and respond to pity's claim, they would sense the great thrill in benevolence. Great as the pleasure is in receiving, greater is the pleasure in benevolence.

There is an old story about a Scotsman, Lord Braco, who was very rich and miserly and who had great stores of gold and silver in his vaults. One day a farmer said to him: "I will give you a shilling if you will but let me see all your gold and silver." Braco consented. The farmer gave him the shilling saying: "Now I am as rich as you are. I have looked at your gold and silver, and that is all you can do with it."

There is more happiness in rejoicing in the good of others, than in rejoicing in our own good. The receiver rejoices in his good; the giver in the joy of others and to such comes the peace nothing in the world can give.

CHAPTER 44

The Problem of Giving

"To HAVE" is the opposite of "to give," yet each of these things
is good in its proper place. To have is to extend our personalities:
we do not contain within ourselves all the essentials for human
living, therefore our "being" must be completed by also "having."
Existence implies the right to have sufficient food and clothing
and a place to live; it does not, however, imply the right to have
a sea-going yacht. Our rights to own property, to have things,
decrease as the objects are farther and farther removed from our
personal necessities.

The virtue of giving is dependent upon having . . . . . for
unless we possess something we cannot give it away. (This is
true even of our time.) But having does not, to most people, appear as an opportunity for giving . . . . . they look upon giving
as a loss, because having is, in itself, so dear to them. This is
short-sighted; if you give away half a loaf, another half-loaf remains to you, and you have had the happiness of being a donor,
too.

Many people, especially among the rich, estimate the value of
their own personalities in terms of owning more and more un-
essential things. They refuse to cut into their capital, increasing
it each year, until it seems to them another self without which
they would not be complete. To slice off a portion of this capital
through alms would seem to them like cutting off an arm or a leg.

One woman has lived in history because she did not fear cutting into her capital. The story is told in the Gospel: *"As He was
sitting opposite the treasury of the temple, Jesus watched the*

multitude throwing coins into the treasury, the many rich with their offerings; and there was one poor widow, who came and put in two mites, which makes a farthing. Thereupon He called his disciples to Him, and said to them, 'Believe me, this poor widow has put in more than all those others who have put offerings into the treasury. The others all gave out of what they had to spare; she, with so little to give, put in all that she had, her whole livelihood.'"

Our Divine Lord was interested in studying the alms-givers and it was the quality of their giving which arrested Him, far more than the quantity they gave. He had once said that where our treasure is, there our heart is, also. Now He tells us that where the heart goes, there the treasure follows. Few of us have His attitude towards alms; we do not trouble to read the list of donors in fine type under the heading, *"Amounts less than . . . . ."* But probably that would be to Him the most important section of the list; on that occasion in the temple He immortalized a gift of two of the smallest coins in the ancient world.

Probably the poor woman at the temple did not see her Judge nor know that she had pleased Him, nor guess that, in the scales of Divine Justice, she *"gave more than all those others who put offerings in the treasury."* They gave of their superfluity: she gave all she had, *"her whole livelihood."* She was poor, yet she gave to the poor. She emptied herself to fill the emptiness of others. The jingle of her two small coins as they fell cried out to refute the whole base philosophy of materialism, which would teach men to acquire as much as they can—as if this earth were our only home.

And the widow's tiny gift has another meaning: it reminds us that Our Lord wants *everything* from us. He was the first "Totalitarian" of the spirit: He asks that we hold nothing back from Him. He demands total love: *"with thy whole mind, thy whole heart, thy whole spirit, and thy whole strength."* Only those who have given their whole hearts to God can give Him their whole capital, as well.

Nothing that is given in such a spirit of generosity is ever lost. In the materialist's reckoning, what is renounced is lost forever.

In the realm of the spirit, this is not true. For what we give to God is not only recorded to us for eternal merit—it is even returned in this life. One of the most practical ways of assuring that we shall always have enough is to give and give and give in the Name of the Lord. Similarly, the most rapid increase in love of God can be obtained by being totally generous to our neighbors. *"Give and the gifts will be yours; good measure, pressed down and shaken up and running over, will be poured into your lap; the measure you award to others is the measure that will be awarded to you."* (Luke 6:39.)

The use to which we put what we have is closely related to what we are, to our "being," and to what we will become. He who keeps everything he has for himself, must lose it all at death; he who has given it away will get it back in the coin of immortality and joy.

CHAPTER 45

The Spirit of Service

THE DESIRE for distinction is one of the most radical principles of our nature; even though it be crucified and buried, in an unexpected moment it revives and rises again in power. The subtle passion is strongest in the middle period of life. It comes in between the love of pleasure which besets youth and the love of gain which besets old age. Opposed to all egotism and selfishness is the ideal of usefulness and service. He only is great of heart who floods the world with great affection; he only is great of mind who stirs the world with pure thoughts. Our Divine Lord gave the key to greatness when He said that He came not to be ministered unto, but to minister. Such service of fellowman as He inspired must be loving in the sense that out of no fountain save that of love can such amazing and endless acts of helpfulness flow.

Loving and serving are inseparable. Such service, too, is self-denying and ego-effacing. To continue helping day after day in the midst of reproach and opposition and rejection means that one is governed by a higher law than the desire of applause of fellowman. Such service cannot be bought, for no gold could purchase it, neither does it need to be bought, for it is freely rendered.

Unless a man sets out to help his neighbor in the spirit of love he will never overcome those faulty tendencies in his nature which constantly try to drag it down. Over 2,000 years ago Aristotle remarked that all of our degrading tendencies arranged themselves under two heads of temper and desire—bad temper and ill-regulated desire. When one is not present the other is, and sometimes one and sometimes the other appear at different periods in the life of the same man. Inasmuch as service is a voluntary undertaking of a work in obedience to the Higher Will, it is a corrective of these tendencies.

It is corrective first of all of temper in its every day form of self-assertion and pride. The man who serves from his heart cannot indulge in egotism. He represses self in order to make his service the more kindly. Each five minutes of conscientious service has the effect of keeping the ego disciplined and of bidding it submit to a Higher and more Righteous Will. Self asserting man always tries to make an inferior feel the full weight of his petty importance and thus, sooner or later, self assertion becomes tyranny. Helpfulness, on the other hand makes the ego appear inferior in order that the neighbor may be exalted.

Irregulated desire is also crushed by affectionate helpfulness. Desire is irregulated when it makes self the center of all things and even the law to which all others must submit. This evil can be cured radically only by making God the object of desire. One then sacrifices many of his luxuries and pleasures in order to assist the needy and the less fortunate. In doing this, character is incidentally improved inasmuch as it detracts one from sensuous and effeminate ease which leads to the spoiling of character.

Even upon material works God has stamped the law of sympathetic service. It is written out in the clouds of the sky to seek to die in the service of rain. The little streams flee decaying self-content by emptying themselves into the vastness of the ocean. The mountains too are in service. They are like giant hands raised to catch and re-distribute the moisture, sending it down across the plains in healthful and life-giving streams. Not a drop of water leads a selfish life; not a wind blast is without its mission. What God has imposed upon nature by law He intended we should impose upon ourselves in virtue of our free will. The waters and the clouds and the mountains and even the earth itself which spends itself in giving life to the seed—all of these rebuke the man who refuses to live for his fellow man. In doing good, everything in God's universe gets good. Service of others is the highest service of self, and the best way for any man to grow in grace is to move forward in helpfulness. The mill wheel will cease to revolve when the waters of the rushing stream are cut off; the moving train stops when the glowing heat cools within the hidden chamber; and charity in this world will degenerate into mere professional schedules and statistical averages without inspiration, without power and without love as men forget the inspiration of Him Who said: "Greater love than this no man hath, that he lay down his life for his friend."

CHAPTER 46

How to Give

"MAKE TO YOURSELF friends with the Mammon of iniquity" is one of the mysterious words of Our Lord to those who do not understand its meaning. "Mammon" is a Syrian word meaning money, and it is called the "Mammon of iniquity" because those to whom Our Lord spoke too often used it for the purposes of injustice and iniquity. A dollar bill in our pocket, if it could speak, might scandalize us in telling us the things for which it was spent, the transactions it had assisted, and the sinful pleasures it had bought. Our Lord tells us that there is a time when it fails, for the man who has money is only a steward. Death says to every man: "Give an account of thy stewardship for thou canst be steward no longer." Money simply cannot be transferred to the world beyond.

Here we come to the purpose of money according to the Saviour. Give away money to those who are in need, for by relieving their necessity you will make friends of those who will intercede for the salvation of your soul. Money will not buy heaven; but it will make friends for us that will help us when we fail. "Inasmuch as you do it to the least of these my brethren, you did it unto me." Those who have been helped by our charity will lead us before the throne saying: "This is he of whom we have spoken and who did so much for us in the life below."

A traveler in a foreign country exchanges his own currency for that of the other land. So too the wealth we have here can be exchanged for spiritual wealth in the next world which "rust does not consume, moths eat, nor thieves break through and steal."

What is the psychology of those who will never touch their capital for charity? They keep piling up more and more reserves, each new addition becoming as sacred as the one before. The answer is that every man is made for the Infinite, which is God. But his reason becomes blinded through prejudice or sin, so he substitutes another infinite which is money. He then wants more and more of *having*, instead of more and more of *being* which is life in God. No matter how many hairs a man has in his head, it hurts to have even one pulled out. No matter how much capital a man has, it hurts to touch even a cent of it. He knows "he can't take it with him" so he denies there is any place to go.

The Christian way is to use money that those who are helped may be our intercessors for heaven. A wealthy man once told his maid to give away fruits in his garden to his neighbors, in order that she might make friends of them. Wealth thus becomes worthy of its name, which is *weal*.

A wealthy woman once got into heaven where St. Peter pointed out the mansion of her chauffeur. She said: "If that is my chauffeur's home, think what mine will be." St. Peter pointed out to her one of the more humble bungalows of heaven saying: "That is your home." "Oh," she said, "I could never live there." St. Peter answered: "Sorry, Madam, but that is the best I could do with the materials you sent me."

There is much money given away, but little of it is used for the soul. Some give it away in order to have their name glorified on the door of a hospital or a university. Men who have had very little education are conspicuous for endowing libraries, that they might create the impression of being learned, which they are not. Our Lord said: "Let not your left hand know what your right hand gives." This was followed by the second principle of giving: The gift must be offered for a Divine reason. The cup of cold water will be given a reward a hundred fold if it is given in Christ's name.

Some years ago the cloister of Carmelite nuns was opened to the public on the feast of St. Theresa. Many curious people poured in to see those women who led a life of silence, prayer and

penance. One man who could not understand their life called
the attention of a young and beautiful nun to the finest residence
in the city which stood on the opposite hill. He said to her:
"Sister, if you could have had that home, with all the wealth,
luxury and pleasure that went with it, would you have left it to
enter the Carmelites?" She answered: "Sir, that was my home."

There is so much giving that is wasted because it is not done
for the soul. The world thinks that the highest things must be
used for the lowest, for example, the intellect to make surplus
wealth. The man of God believes that the lowest must be used
for the highest, that is, money must be spent to help spread
Divine Truth, to solace the afflicted and to cure the sick that their
souls may be free to work out their salvation. The truest answer
to "You can't take it with you" is: "You can, provided you give it
away." Then it is stored up as merit in the next life.

FELLOWSHIP

CHAPTER 47

The Divine Psychology of Gossip

TRADITIONALLY, all gossips are women; but men are often guilty of the same offense. They call it "judging."

Our Divine Lord, in speaking of gossips, said: "Do not judge others, or you yourselves will be judged." His admonition not to "judge" demands that we make no wicked evaluations, do not look for the worst in others. God alone sees our neighbor's heart; we see only his face. In England the judges wear wigs in court, to show that it is the law which is passing judgment, and not their own personal views. This is done in recognition of the truth all men suspect—that there is something impudent in allowing even the wisest among us to engage in pigeon-holing our friends or cataloguing our enemies.

When we judge others, we also judge ourselves. Our Lord asked us not to judge, lest we be judged; and sometimes the judgment we make of others is in itself a condemnation of our own faults. When one woman calls another "catty," she reveals that she knows what cattiness involves. Jealousy can be a tribute paid by mediocrity to genius: the jealous person then admits the superiority of his rival but since he cannot reach that level himself, he drags the other down to his. Other forms of criticism are equally revealing of the one who criticizes.

Our Lord told us that the gossip's faults are often greater than those he criticizes in his neighbor. "How is it that thou canst see the speck of dust which is in thy brother's eye, and are not aware of the beam that is thy own? By what right wilt thou say to thy brother, Brother, let me rid thy eye of that speck, when thou canst not see the beam that is in thy own? Thou hypocrite, take the beam out of thy own eye first, and so thou shalt have clear sight to rid thy brother's of the speck."

The "speck" was only a bit of chaff, a splinter of wood. But the beam was a sizable piece of timber. To set ourselves up as worthy of judging others is already to see ourselves as their superiors, to be guilty of the sin of pride, the huge "beam" that obscures our vision. We cannot gossip without either over-rating ourselves or under-rating our neighbors . . . and frequently we do both. For the gossip is prone to project onto another the fault he suspects within himself. No one gets angrier at being told a lie than an habitual liar. The incurable gossip flies into a rage when he hears that he, in turn, has been talked about behind his back.

Our Lord asked the gossips to examine their own right to condemn the faults of others. "He that is without sin among you, let him cast the first stone." The implication is clear: innocence alone has the right to condemn. But innocence will always wish to take on the guilt of the other, to atone for his failings as if they were his own. Love recognizes the sin, but love also dies for it.

We instinctively feel that the abuse of our neighbors is wrong, and we show it by the words we use when we are about to cut somebody's throat. For they are words of self-apology: "One doesn't like to be uncharitable, but . . . ," or, "Of course, we mustn't criticize, but . . . ," or "I always prefer not to judge anyone, but . . . ." These words presage the knife . . . and the effect on him who has wielded it is always psychological darkness. "He that loveth his brother abideth in light. . . . But he that hateth his brother is in darkness."

God has offered a beautiful reward to those who do not judge: they themselves shall not be judged when they are brought before the heavenly court. Yet God's judgment—which they will escape—is sure to be more merciful than any that we make. David, when he had sinned, was asked whether he would rather receive his punishment from God or from man; and he wisely chose God's judgment as offering the greater mercy.

We men and women are not wise enough nor innocent enough to judge each other. And the only decision we can rightly make about our brother who is doing wrong is to admit it and to say, "We will leave him to God."

CHAPTER 48

Atomic Men

As FEAR grips the world, one truth cries out for repetition: it is not atomic bombs that we need fear, but atomic men—the men who have built a civilization in which bombs might be used. It is always the human agent who is responsible for acts of war, and not a lifeless weapon; a bow and arrow in the hands of a professional archer is not the menace it would have been in the hands of a wild Indian.

The forces of nature know no morality; it is men who use or abuse their powers. Electricity is useful—but not if every place where one sits down is turned into an electric chair. Fire is a blessing when we use it to cook a meal, a curse when the arsonist uses it to burn a house. The remedies in a drug-store relieve us when the druggist is an ethical man; but in the hands of a criminal they would be immensely dangerous. Thus, too, the atomic bomb is not a threat to anyone. It is men who threaten our safety.

But why *do* men expend their energies in the ugly task of trying to destroy mankind? The answer can be found in a word that applies to our times: devolution. The modern world has little to say today about evolution, whose enthusiasts once supposed that human progress was automatic and sure. Men are not so pleased with their own performance today that they dwell smugly on their imagined origin as apes. But if evolution has lost its hold on popular thought, devolution has been all too sadly substantiated. And this is indicated by the fact that, as man gained mastery over nature, he lost mastery over his own nature. Modern man is the victim of his own inventions.

The devolution of man has passed through three stages, similar to those we see in the case of a son who turns aside from the devoted father who—through kindness, love and mercy—tries to inspire his obedience to the moral law.

The first stage is one of indifference: the son drifts away from his father and ignores his teachings, which he regards as undue restraints upon his freedom to do whatever pleases him. "The old man is behind the times," is his slogan at this period.

In the second stage, as the son intensifies the immorality of his living, indifference changes into hatred. He no longer thinks of his father *as* a father, but discounts his very humanity, saying, "The old man is a crack-pot." In the third stage, this hatred of his father expands to become hatred of the whole world, and the rebellious young man complains, "Nobody understands me." His conscience makes it impossible for him to live at peace with himself and, as a consequence, he cannot live at peace with anybody else.

These correspond to the three stages of devolution, by which man has fallen away from loving his Heavenly Father. In the first stage, man denies the existence of God. Finding the Divine commandments an uncomfortable curb on his way of living, he rationalizes his misconduct by saying, "God is only a myth." In the second stage, man denies the essence of God: he sees God as an enemy. The Pharisees said that Our Lord was a Devil; they interpreted the essence of God as Wickedness, rather than as Goodness. Thus, the Communists today do not deny God (as the bourgeois atheists may do), but they fight against God with an *active* atheism, which, not denying His existence, struggles to destroy Him.

In the third stage, hatred of God expands into hatred of our fellowmen. The man who has tried to kill God always goes further and tries to kill his neighbor, for those who sever the first bond of love cannot rest until they have broken all the rest. The Spanish have a proverb: "He who spits against Heaven, spits in his own face." The exile of God from a civilization necessarily leads to cruel and tyrannical relationships among its members. And the hatred of our fellowmen, which results from denial of God's love, finds its final physical expression in the atomic bomb: the man who could not live with God now finds he cannot share the earth with other men.

The answer does not lie in "atomic control." It is to be found in human control. When school boys throw stones at windows, we do not seek to discipline the stones; it is boy-control that is our problem. International organizations cannot prevent lethal hell from breaking loose until man reverses himself and begins again to love and to serve God—and this is a job each man must do alone, a job that "conferences" cannot accomplish.

There is only one way of banishing enmity from the world: men cannot learn to love their neighbors, much less their enemies, until they first return to love of God Himself. Then—recognizing that He made everyone and finds each human being dear to Him —we shall be able to love all men, too.

"Practical" men may object that it is indiscreet for one-half of the world to return to God, while the other half continues to hate Him. This is like being fearful of a small child's transparent plan to trip me on the stairs, when his father, who sees everything, and never lets him out of sight, is there to loosen the string. We do not need to fear the malice of hearts open to God's inspection, as all human hearts are. For if God is on our side, what does it matter who tries to act against us?

MAN

CHAPTER 49

Progress

G. K. CHESTERTON once said: "There is one thing in the world that never makes any progress and that is the idea of progress." By this he meant that unless we have a fixed concept of what progress really means we can never know that we are making any headway. Unfortunately, there are many who, instead of working toward an ideal, change it, and call it progress. One would never know he was making progress from Chicago to San Francisco if San Francisco became identified with New York. Only when the goal is fixed and definite do we ever have a target and the energy to shoot the arrow.

Everything in earth's geology and everything on the earth's surface point to a future: the impulse of a river is forward into the sea; the little child tells what he intends to be when he is a man; thoughts fly on wings toward the tomorrow; all these impulses which carry us onward imply a future under God. Those who lose sight of the goal often concentrate on mere motion and try to derive pleasure from it. They delight in turning the pages of a book, but never finish the story; they pick up brushes, but never finish a picture; they travel the seas, but know no ports. Their zest is not in the achievement of a destiny but rather in gyration and action for the mere sake of movement.

Perfection is being, not doing; it is not to affect an act but to achieve a character. There is nothing that makes life unhappier than its meaninglessness, and life is devoid of meaning only when it is without purpose. There are tens of thousands of minor purposes, but the one great purpose is the perfection of our character from a moral point of view. Infinite as are the varities of life, he who has not found out directly how to make everything converge to the sanctification of his own soul has missed the meaning of life.

The son of Confucius once said to him: "I apply myself with diligence to every kind of study, and neglect nothing that could render me clever and ingenious, but still I do not advance." To which Confucius answered: "Omit some of your pursuits and you will get on better." The life of a man is vagrant, changeful, desultory, like that of children chasing butterflies, until he has discovered for himself why he is here and where he is going. Rivers do not grow shallower as they roll away from their sources, and the heart's river need not be any exception. It should flow on, widening and deepening until it meets the great ocean of Divine Love for which it is destined, and mingles with it.

Dissatisfaction sometimes can be the motive of true progress. Dissatisfied with the pen, man invented the printing press; dissatisfied with the chariot and the locomotive, he invented the airplane. There is implanted in everyone an impulse which drives the spirit to beat its wings like an imprisoned eagle in the cages of this earth until there is blood on its plumes. Did hearts but analyze this urge that is within them, which drives them away from the actual to the possible and makes them dig in the desert of their lives for new living springs, and climb every mountain to get a better look at heaven, they would see that they are being drawn back again to God, from Whom they came.

To stay complacently where we are in our spiritual life is to be as a tree that might congratulate itself that it is higher than the shrubs, or to be like a caterpillar that should stay exultant with its spots and stripes whilst the glorious life of the butterfly is untasted. No man is living who is resting on his own laurels, as no one is happy who says that he lives on his memories. Past laurels must be put aside as man must press forward to that supernal vocation to which he is called, forgetting the things that are behind. The bird must forget its nest, the sea its husk, the flower its bud, and unless these are forgotten we can never reach the goal. Both brooding and boasting are alike to be discouraged, for the happiness of life is in the prospect of the best and the holiest.

CHAPTER 50

The Mass-Man

A NEW TYPE OF MAN is multiplying in the modern world, and if there be any reader who recognizes his own portrait herein, let him take pause, reflect, and change. The new man is the mass-man, who no longer prizes his individual personality, but who seeks to be submerged in the collectivity or crowd.

This mass-man may be recognized by the following traits:

1) He is without originality of judgment; does no other reading except what is found in a daily newspaper, or picture magazine, or an occasional novel. He has only a different point of view to give on a common subject, but no new principle or solution.

2) He hates tranquility, meditation, silence or anything which gives him leisure to penetrate into the depths of his soul. He needs noise, crowds, and the radio, whether he listens to the latter or not.

3) Evasion or escape from self is a necessity. Alcohol, cocktails, detective stories, or movies are taken in steady doses to fill up the emptiness of the hour. As the genius loves concentration, he seeks dispersion, particularly sex, in order that the excitement of the moment may dispel consideration of the problem of life.

4) He seeks to be influenced rather than to influence, is sensitive to propaganda, to the excitations of publicity and generally has one favorite columnist who does his thinking for him.

5) He believes that every instinct should be satisfied, regardless of whether or not its exercise is in accordance with right reason; he cannot understand self-denial, or self-discipline; he regards

self-expression as identical with freedom, and at no vital points is he master of himself.

6) His beliefs of right and wrong change like the weather-cock; he maintains positions which are nothing but a succession of contradictions, lays down mental tracks one month and the next month pulls them up. He is going nowhere, but he is sure he is on the way. He has no sense of gratitude toward the past and no sense of responsibility to the future. Nothing matters but distractions, so that life becomes cut up into a crazy pattern of successive instants none of which add up to make sense.

7) He identifies money and pleasure, and hence seeks to have much of the first in order to have much of the second. But the money must be obtained with as little effort as possible. The ego is the center of everything and everything is to be related to it through the intermediary of money.

8) To break his solitude he has recourse to an ersatz communion with others, through night clubs, parties and collective distractions. But from each of these he returns more lonely than before, finally believing with Sartre that "hell is others."

9) Being a mass-man completely standardized, he hates superiority in others, either real or imagined. Scandals he loves because they seem to prove that others are no better than he. Religion he dislikes, the real reason being that by denying it he thinks he could then go on living as he does without remorse of conscience.

10) He might just as well go by a number as by a name he is so immersed in the crowd mind. Even the authority he invokes is anonymous. It is always "they." "They say," or "they are wearing," or "they are doing this." Anonymity becomes a protection against the assuming of responsibilities. In the big cities he feels more free because he is less known, but at the same time he hates it because it cancels his personal distinction. The perfect symbol of the impersonal mass-man is the social security number, which completes his alienation from himself.

These are the ten marks of the mass-man who is the raw material of every form of Totalitarianism from Fascism to Communism. Psychologically, he is also the unhappy man, full of despair, anxiety, fear, and afraid of the meaninglessness of life. But he is not hopeless if he would but enter into himself. The only reason he wants to be lost in the crowd is because he cannot bear his inner misery. It follows that he must detach himself from the masses and come to grips with himself. Flight is cowardice and escapism, especially flight into anonymity.

It takes a brave man to look into the mirror of his own soul to see written there the disfigurements caused by his own misbehavior. It is no truism to say men must be men, not atoms in a mass. Once man sees his self-inflicted wounds, the next step is to take them to the Divine Physician to be cured. It was to such tired mass-men that He made His appeal: "Come to Me all ye who labor and are heavily burdened and find rest for your souls."

CHAPTER 51

A Recall to the Inner Life

A FATHER gave his little son a cut-up puzzle of the world and asked him to put it together. The boy finished the picture in an amazingly short time. When the astonished father asked him how he did it, the boy answered: "There was a picture of a man on the other side; when I put the man together, the world came out all right." Such is the key to the understanding of all the political and economic problems of our day. Nothing ever happens to the world which does not first happen inside man. Wars are not made by politics, but by politicians with a certain philosophy of life. No explanation of war has ever been as clear as the Biblical one which declares that wars are punishments on man for his sin. Not a punishment in the sense that God sends a war as a father spanks a child for an act of disobedience; but rather that a war follows a breakdown of morality, as thunder follows lightning, and as blindness follows the plucking out of the eye.

Those who are in middle age have lived through an era where war is more "normal" than peace. There has been literally fulfilled what Nietszche prophesied, namely, that the twentieth century would be a century of wars. War is a symptom of the breakdown of civilization. There are only different degrees of guilt among the combatants. All is not black on one side, and all is not white on another. When a body becomes diseased, the germ does not localize in one organ to the exclusion of all others; it infects the whole blood stream. So the evil of our day is the evil not of the East or the West, but of the world. It is of the world because men generally have become estranged from the true center of their spiritual life. Having ceased to fear God, in the sense of filial fear such as a child has for a father, they have begun to fear man with a servile fear, such as a slave has for a tyrant.

Modern man has become passive in the face of evil. He has so long preached a doctrine of false tolerance; has so long believed that right and wrong were only differences in a point of view, that now when evil works itself out in practice he is paralyzed to do anything against it. Political injustice, chicanery in high office, and organized crime leave him cold. While keeping very busy and active on the outside, he is passive and inert on the inside, because he rarely enters into his own heart. Remedying the evil therefore falls to agencies and mechanical realities external to man. No government or state can put the screws on personal freedom, unless the citizens have already abdicated in themselves the basis of that freedom, namely, their responsibility to God.

Having lost his inward unity, man is more and more compelled to seek the unity outside himself in the unity of organization. Disclaiming all responsibility, he surrenders it more and more to the State. The sheep that will not obey the shepherd must be retrieved by a dog barking at their heels. The citizen who will not obey the moral laws of God, must be organized by a dictator snapping at their souls. The weakening of the inner spiritual life is the basic cause of the disharmony and discord which prevail throughout the world. The forcible organization of the chaos created by the enfeeblement of the moral sense always calls forth some dictator who makes law personal rather than a reflection of the Eternal harmony that rules in the heavens.

A great burden is thrust upon men who call themselves religious. In this fatal hour, all of their energies should be spent recalling man to his spiritual destiny and summoning him to invoke the God Who made him. Instead of that there are some who would accuse their neighbors who also believe in God, of being disloyal to their country, or else of trying to impose their faith by force on their fellow citizens. Such lies do a disservice both to God and to country. And their supposed faith in God is to be questioned, because no one who loves God hates his neighbor, nor does he try to incite citizen against citizen through slander. Let those who call themselves Catholics, or Protestants, or Jews recall that the function of their religion is to intensify the spiritual life of man and not to empty the vials of bitterness into hearts, stirring up one against another. It is not to the politicians and the economists and the social reformers that we must look for the first steps in this spiritual recovery; it is to the professed religious. The non-religious can help by repudiating those who come to them in the name of God or America and say that their neighbor does not love either. Religion must not be a cloak covering the dagger of hate!

CHAPTER 52

Sneeze Morality

THERE IS A TENDENCY among many shallow thinkers of our day to teach that every human act is a reflex, over which we do not exercise human control. They would rate a generous deed as no more praiseworthy than a wink, a crime as no more voluntary than a sneeze. Men are believed, by such false thinkers, to be "conditioned" to act this way or that—with no freedom of choice, no responsibility for their good deeds or bad. They tell us that crime and sin are caused by an insufficiency of playgrounds or by a childhood shock which turned the child into a "problem child" and prevented his ever "adjusting" to reality and its demands.

Such a philosophy undercuts all human dignity. It confuses conduct, which is human, with behavior, which is animal. It ignores the spiritual faculties of man, which enable him to act against his impulses, to refuse the course of least resistance because of his allegiance to an ideal. This false conception of human nature contradicts our own common-sense experience: you do not *have* to finish reading this column, nor do you *have* to set it aside. You are conscious, now, of your freedom to follow one course or the other in the next three minutes. All of us have the power of choice in action at every moment of our lives.

"I couldn't help doing it," is the weakest and least likely of excuses. It is particularly favored by liars: they say, "She asked my opinion of her new hat, and I couldn't tell her the truth!" Why not? The truth need never offend if it is told with charity and friendliness. "I simply *had* to" is not a valid excuse for committing any sin, and lying is a sin.

The notion that men act because of "forces" stronger than their wills leads to great dangers in the social scene. Even killing is justified by some, who say that economic necessity makes wars inevitable. No one in the age of faith ever spoke of wars as a necessity. Wars are made by men, not by economies, and men, in saner ages than our own, were known to be free agents, deciding their own destinies.

St. James told us, "What leads to war, what leads to quarreling among you? I will tell you what leads to them: the appetites that infest your mortal bodies. Your desires go unfulfilled, so you fall to murdering; you set your heart on something, and cannot have your will, so there is quarreling and fighting."

Atomic warfare is not "sure" to come; men will decide in their hearts whether such a war will come or not. The lifeless bomb does not create the problem of our times: men's cruelty creates our problem. A stock-pile of bombs in the hands of St. Francis of Assisi would be as harmless as a flower. But a single bomb in the hands of a Soviet dictator (or of a President willing to release it) can menace New York or prove a scandalous calamity to Hiroshima.

Christian tradition attributes evil to a personal choice, an act of the free will which misuses the liberty that God gave to man. Freedom is vastly prized today in the speeches of politicians, but it is only political freedom which they praise; nobody takes the microphone to remind the individual listener that he is morally free, that his sins are of his making. Such liberty is derided: we sometimes have to sneeze. Therefore, according to the confused thinkers, we have to sin and nothing can prevent it. This effort to deny man's freedom would, if it could succeed, turn people into so many animals.

The "sneeze morality" recommends itself particularly to those who wish to escape the voice of conscience. They long to believe in a philosophy which will allow them to be cruel and untruthful and proud without a sense of guilt. Their own consciences, their uncorrupted reasons, tell them that what they are doing is wrong and that they will be held accountable for it. To escape this uncomfortable knowledge, some of them attempt to bribe their consciences into bringing in a more favorable report. They set up a new morality, gauged to fit their actions and to measure them as good. Since the true conscience has caused discomfort, they will devise a false conscience to reassure and flatter them.

The man who has created a new conscience in this manner has set himself up as a rival to God, able to determine right and wrong. When he does something good (such as contributing to a charity and getting his name in the papers for it) he takes full credit. When he does something bad, he says, "It is because I am built that way," or "My childhood was unhappy, so I cannot be expected to behave."

False consciences seem to succeed—but only in the daylight hours. Even sneeze moralists, in the long nights, know remorse—and their uneasiness is the Voice of God, summoning them away from their self-made slavery to the glorious freedom of the children of God.

CHAPTER 53

What Makes Us Normal

Unless we have a clear idea of what it is to be normal, we shall never know when we have departed from the standard of mental and moral health. And so an understanding of how a human being "works" . . . and ought to "work" . . . will help us to catch ourselves, in time, and put a stop to our tendencies towards abnormality.

Every single human movement passes through three stages. First, there is a thought. Next, an emotional response. Finally, an act.

The *idea* always comes before the emotion. A daughter's tears do not cause her mother's death; it is the death which occasions the tears. Thus the mind registers experience, as it becomes aware of events in the world about us; then, like a captain on the bridge of a ship, it signals the event to the body which is under its control, like orders going to a ship's engine-room. The body responds with the appropriate emotion.

We may think of our bodies (which include our emotions) as musical instruments upon which the mind of a man may play whatever tune he wishes. For the kind of thoughts we allow into our minds determine the kind of feelings we will later have. Worry can cause ulcers, and the thought of something fearful can drive blood to the active muscles, causing them to tense.

Emotions normally lead us to action, and so become discharged; for actions are the third or final stage, of which an idea was the first. In even the simplest actions the process is clear: a spectator at a football game may swerve his body towards an opening which the player does not see. The idea of the opening brought about a wish to see it filled (the emotion), and the body's action followed the wish and the idea!

When we once know this much about ourselves, we can use the facts in everyday life. We see, at once, the absurdity of saying, "It makes no difference how you think; all that matters is how you live." For we act on our beliefs, and if our ideas are wrong, so will our actions be. To desire evil is to prepare ourselves for evil deeds: "He who casts his eyes on a woman so as to lust after her has already committed adultery in his heart."

And if our creed is wrong, our behavior will err. If we have not discovered true answers to the question of why we are here and where we are going, we cannot feel or act with certainty or with consistency. The man who does not think straight will neither feel happy nor act rightly, for the idea is the source of all he feels and does.

Sometimes wrong ideas slip past our guard; they may even reach the second stage of emotional attraction before we are able to arrest them. But usually we can catch an idea in its first stage, and should, if it is a wrong or unhealthy idea, always try to banish it from our minds at once. It is always best to watch it early, before it begets an emotion: the mind must be as careful of the ideas on which it feeds as the stomach is of the food it absorbs. Yet many people who would never dream of serving garbage at their tables will welcome garbage-literature and garbage-moving-pictures into their minds.

Ideas and emotions should not be repressed . . . that is, they should not be pushed out of consciousness through fear or guilt or an unwillingness to admit that "someone like me" could ever have such thoughts. Ideas that run counter to the moral law and the Christian ideal should be expelled from the mind calmly, and with no more flurry than we would use in rejecting an undigestible piece of food which is offered us.

If an idea which is evil reaches the emotional stage, we can still dispose of it, and without either repressing it (which is dangerous) or expressing it in action (which is usually worse). We can express the emotional energy the idea has given us, *but in the opposite direction*, so that it becomes a force of good.

Suppose, for instance that a man employed by a bank has a strong temptation to effect a robbery, and that he finds his heart beating in anticipation of the pleasures such a theft would buy for him. If he dwells on the idea in morbid fear, he will paralyze all his normal actions. If he submits to the temptation, he will find stealing becoming a habit, for "appetite grows by what it feeds on". But there is a way out: he can channel his energy into a useful direction. Instead of letting his mind contrive methods of defrauding the bank, he can use the same mental energy to increase his efficiency and, eventually, win for his honest own the money he had begun to covet.

Evil thoughts are best destroyed by good thoughts that crowd them, evil loves by stronger loves of the good. St. Paul says, "Be not overcome by evil, but overcome evil by good." Evil is not to be fought, head-on, by mere brute will-power; it is better for us to flank it, to drive it from the field by a greater intensity of goodness, a greater love for God. A mind filled with ideas of love and beauty has little room for evil notions.

CHAPTER 54

How to Overcome Bad Habits

"I HAVE a bad temper," or "I drink too much"—"I am always criticizing," or "I am lazy" are familiar complaints from those who still believe that nobility of character is an important goal. They would not make such admissions if they did not have a strong desire to break the chain of evil habits. They can realize this desire—any bad habit can be broken. But getting free of it requires four things:

Introspection is necessary in order that we shall isolate the habit and see it clearly as a sin. The surprise we feel when others criticize some fault in us proves that we have not practiced introspection sufficiently to know ourselves. Some people are afraid ever to look into their consciences, for fear of what they might find; they are like the other cowards who dare not open telegrams because they dread bad news. But introspection is to the soul what diagnosis is to the body—the first necessary step toward health. The Prodigal Son "entered into himself" before he was able to resolve to admit his mistakes to his father. Turning the search-light of attention upon ourselves shows us the vice or evil habit which requires correction; it makes us see ourselves not as we wish we were, but as we really are.

Avoiding the occasions of sin is the easiest way of avoiding sin itself. The way to keep out of trouble is to keep out of the situations that lead up to trouble: the man who gets burned whenever he is near a fire had better eschew fires. The alcoholic must avoid the first sip of the first drink; the libertine must keep away from pretty women, the evil-minded must flee the company of those who degrade him. Our Lord said, "He that loveth the danger will perish therein." Temptation is hard to overcome at the last moment, when the sin is within our reach; it is easy to overcome if we act decisively to avoid a situation in which we might be tempted. Environments can make sin repulsive or attractive to us, for our surroundings affect us all. But we can *choose* the environment we wish and can ruthlessly reject the one that leads to trouble. Our Lord told us, "If thy right eye is the occasion of thy falling into sin, pluck it out and cast it away from thee." This means that if the books we read, the homes we visit, the games we play cause us to stumble morally, then we should cut them out and cast them from us.

An act of the will is vital to any accomplishment. Doctors tell us that nothing is a greater help to the sick than a will to live. So, if we are to overcome our vices, we must bring a strong will to bear on them. We acquired the bad habits only because we gave ground to them by a consent of the will, until they became automatic and perhaps even unconscious. To master them, we must reverse the process and use the will to break their automatic functioning. Our characters do not consist in what we know, but in what we choose, and choosing is done by the will. After the Prodigal had entered into himself and left the environment of sin, his next step was to brace himself with the great resolve, "I will arise and go to my father."

A right philosophy of life is needed to complete the work, for evil habits cannot be overcome by the will alone: love is required as well. No alcoholic is cured until he finds something to value more highly than the attractions of alcohol. No other evil is renounced until the sinner finds some positive good he prizes above his sin. Our Lord warned us of the house, swept and garnished, which was filled by seven devils worse than the first; this was the inevitable result when an evil was driven out but no good was sent to take its place. Even in the moral world, nature abhors a vacuum.

Evil habits are not driven out by our hate of them (for we do not always hate them properly). They are crowded out by our love of something else. The new love that takes possession of us must be bigger than ourselves . . . for it is our selves which need amendment. It cannot safely be anything earthly that we use as a substitute love; the man who cures himself of dissipation through pride or ambition may be worse off, in his reform, than in his sin. No new, competing love is large enough except the love of God Himself, with all that that love makes us long to do. St. Augustine summarized its effects when he said, "Love God, and do what you will." For if you love God truly, you will never wish to hurt Him, any more than you would wish to hurt a human friend.

Habits cannot be efficaciously fought unless we have a philosophy which makes our lives revolve around the God for Whom we are made, and without Whom we are miserably bound to the drab companionship of our own growing imperfections.

CHAPTER 55

Readiness for Sacrifice

Never before in a period of truce (for we can hardly call our times "peaceful") has there been so great a readiness for sacrifice as today. This spirit is not yet overt and manifest; it is still hidden, like water under the surface of the earth.

The potential for sacrifice is shown in two ways: one of them morbid and masochistic, the other healthy and hopeful. The symptom of the first kind of sacrifice is the submission to Totalitarianism of almost one-quarter of the earth's peoples. Communism offers a secular version of the Christian doctrine of sacrifice. It announces that self-denial, purges, liquidation, the violence of revolution are needed before man can enter into a new kind of heaven upon earth. Communism has found many who subscribe to it—not because its teachings are true, but because men had wearied of the milk-and-water Liberalism which knew no evil wicked enough to condemn and no good high enough to be worth dying for. Communism is filling the vacuum created by the abandonment of the Divine plea: *"Take up your cross daily and follow me."*

But there are healthier signs of a yearning for sacrifice: the demands of youth for something hard and worthwhile doing. Those among them who have found a "cause" serve it tirelessly, so long as they believe that it is going to help the world. If it be objected that other young men and women turn to social anarchy and carnal license, I would say that this is no proof of youth's weakness, nor of their rebellion against law and authority. I see it rather as a protest against the weakness of their elders, who watered truth with error, virtue with vice, and diluted the drama out of life. The revolutionary spirit of our young people is a protest against their elders' failure to pass on to them sharp, clear values worth fighting for; their revolt is a gesture of contempt for the passive barbarism of the society into which they have been born. Their carnal license is a rebellion against the emptiness of life, lived with only selfish ends in view; they try to compensate for its lack of meaning by the intensity of erotic experiences. Even in the worst indictments of youth we can see a hope: these things indicate a reaching-out toward a larger destiny and a life of dedication.

One period of Roman history has many similarities to our own; men in those days chose as their philosophy stoicism, which had as its ideal, *"Grit your teeth and bear it."* In modern times another philosophy, even less satisfying to man's spirit than the Roman Stoicism, was born out of the crises of our two World Wars. It appeared first in Germany after World War I, and in France in our own day; it is known as Existentialism.

Stoicism prepared men for social nihilism, the decay of civilization; Existentialism bids men accept an inner nihilism, the decay of the human personality which has abandoned God. Existentialist philosophers do, at least, see clearly when they ask men to choose between the two supreme alternatives: God or nothing. When one has reached that choice, he cannot remain on the level of mediocrity: such a man goes down to insanity and suicide, or up to God through sacrifice and self-denial.

The great majority of people today—especially young people —are ready for the high ascent; it is their leaders who fail them. Themselves brought up in an atmosphere of Dilutionism—which tried to streamline the Cross and soften its jagged edges so that they would not hurt—they are unprepared to satisfy the deeper cravings of a cross-hungry people. Superficial observers may think that the popular leader is the one who promises something for nothing—years of vacations with pay, pensions for workers at thirty; but the future leader who will really capture the imagination of Americans, especially of our youth, will wear a cross on his back.

The days for leading men with promises are at an end. The time for leading them through appeals for heroism, sacrifice and self-denial have begun. Millions will flock to the banners of the man who gives the people something better worth loving than themselves. Calvary seemed far away in the days when automatic progress seemed assured; it has come closer and enlarged its appeal in a decade of adversity. The new America longs for an opportunity to sacrifice selfish interests in a worthy cause. Once leaders arise who are themselves willing victims in a sacrifice for the best we know, we shall have good times for everyone.

CHAPTER 56

Does Mercy Stand Alone?

As the world grows soft, it uses more and more the word *mercy*. This could be a praiseworthy characteristic if mercy were understood aright. But too often by mercy is meant letting off anyone who breaks the natural or the Divine law, or who betrays his country. Such mercy is an emotion, not a virtue, when it justifies the killing by a son of his father because he is "too old." To avoid any imputation of guilt, what is actually a murder is called *euthanasia*.

Forgotten in all such mercy pleas is the principle that *mercy is the perfection of justice*. Mercy does not come first, and then justice; but rather justice first, then mercy. The divorce of mercy from justice is sentimentality, as the divorce of justice from mercy is severity. Mercy is not love when it is divorced from justice. He who loves anything must resist that which would destroy the object of his love. The power to become righteously indignant is not an evidence of the want of mercy and love, but rather a proof of it. There are some crimes the tolerance of which is equivalent to consent to their wrong. Those who ask for the release of murderers, traitors, and the like, on the grounds that we must be "merciful, as Jesus was merciful," forget that that same Merciful Saviour also said that He came not to bring peace, but the sword. As a mother proves that she loves her child by hating the physical disease which would ravage the child's body, so Our Lord proves He loved Goodness by hating evil, which would ravage the souls of His creatures. For a doctor to be merciful to typhoid germs or polio in a patient, or for a judge to be tolerant of rape, would be in a lower category the same as for Our Lord to be indifferent to sin. A mind that is never stern or indignant is either without love, or else is dead to the distinction between right and wrong.

Love can be stern, forceful, and even fierce, as was the love of the Saviour. It makes a scourge of ropes and drives buyers and sellers out of temples; it refuses to give the courtesy of speech to moral triflers like Herod, for it would only add to his moral guilt; it turns on a Roman Procurator, boasting of Totalitarian law, and reminds him that he would have no power unless it were given to him by God. When a gentle hint to a woman at the well did no good, He went to the point ruthlessly and reminded her that she had five divorces. When so-called righteous men would put Him out of the way, He tore the mask off their hypocrisy and called them a "brood of vipers." When He heard of the shedding of the blood of the Galileans, it was with formidable harshness that He said: "You will all perish as they did, if you do not repent." Equally stern was He to those who would offend the little ones with an education that was progressive in evil: "If anyone hurts the conscience of one of these little ones that believe in me, he had better been drowned in the depths of the sea, with a mill-stone tied about his neck." He told men to pluck out eyes and cut off hands and feet, rather than to allow these members to become occasions for evil and the occasion of the loss of their immortal souls. When one of His disciples asked to be excused from his apostolic work to bury his father, Our Lord said: "Do thou follow Me, and leave the dead bury their dead." While Martha waited on Him at table, he pointed out that something else was needed more than service. When His apostles slept, He awakened them ruthlessly and chided them for their want of prayer; and in spite of Thomas's full confession, He rebuked him for his want of faith. One of His looks was so soul-piercing, revealing the weakness and evil within, that a disciple was moved to tears.

If mercy meant the forgiveness of all faults without retribution and without justice, it would end in the multiplication of wrongs. Mercy is for those who will not abuse it, and no man will abuse it who has already started to make the wrong right, as justice demands. What some today call mercy is not mercy at all, but a feather-bed for those who fall from justice; and thus they multiply guilt and evil by supplying such mattresses. To become the object of mercy is not the same as to go scot-free, for as the word of God says: "Whom the Lord loveth, He chastiseth." The moral man is not he who is namby-pamby, or who has drained his emotions of the sterner stuff of justice; rather he is one whose gentleness and mercy are part of a larger organism, whose eyes can flash with righteous indignation, and whose muscles can become as steel in defense, like Michael, of the Justice and the Rights of God.

CHAPTER 57

Why We Are Not Better

THE REASON why we are not better than we are is that we do not *will* to be better: the sinner and the saint are set apart only by a series of tiny decisions within our hearts. Opposites are never so close as in the realm of the spirit: an abyss divides the poor from the rich, and one may cross it only with the help of external circumstances and good fortune. The dividing line between ignorance and learning is also deep and wide: both leisure to study and a gifted mind would be required to turn an ignoramus into a learned man. But the passage from sin to virtue, from mediocrity to sanctity requires no "luck," no help from outer circumstances. It can be achieved by an efficacious act of our own wills in cooperation with God's grace.

St. Thomas tells us that, "We are not saints because we *will* not to be saints." He does not say, mind you, that we do not *want* to be saints: many of us do. But mere *wanting* is the wish that something shall come to pass without our acting to bring it about. *Willing* means that we plan to pay the necessary cost in effort and in sacrifice.

We often delude ourselves into imagining that we have willed to be better, when we have made actually many reservations, have determined there are many present practices we will not change; then the willing is merely an idle wish. The key to spiritual advancement is to be found in the Creed: *"He descended into hell; the third day He arose again."* Each of us, too, must make a descent into the subconsciousness, to the portions of our minds which we keep dark, for it is here that the unspoken reservations hide. These reservations are not easily seen by us, but they color everything that we do see; they act like so many colored windows, changing the truth of external reality as it reaches our conscious minds. Reality is distorted if we have such reservations as prejudice, habits of sin, pride, avarice and jealousy; any of these can make honest judgment impossible for us. The truth is then twisted to fit our imperfections; we lie to ourselves in order not to have to change, not to abandon these prized habits of evil.

Most of us live out our lives with a false picture of ourselves which we will not surrender; we dread the pain of finding ourselves less noble than we like to believe. We strain reality through a sieve of self-love, keeping out whatever truth would hurt us. Using this private measurement of truth is as misguided as it would be to let our own preferences decide which key on the piano is middle C . . . . and as useless. We might pretend that a key easier to reach was middle C, and act accordingly; but we should make discords, instead of harmonies. Reality cannot be cowed to fit our wishes.

These reservations to which we cling . . . . these attitudes we insist we will not surrender or change . . . . affect our conscious judgments and make them untrue. Before we can ever emerge into the gladness of God's reality, we have to go down into the hell in which we hide these unadmitted faults. This requires us to make a thoroughgoing analysis of ourselves in the light of God's unchanging laws.

The "Don't kid yourself!" of slang is sound spiritual advice. Nothing so stands in the way of our progress towards God as egotism, and the egotist is always full of self-deceit, of "sacred" faults he will not renounce, nor even admit he has. That is why the egotist in all of us requires a pitless searching-out of every hidden nook and corner of our minds. We need to see the self as it really is, and not as we pretend it is. We must love Truth more than we love self; we must be willing to surrender all our unguessed faults, if we are ever to be able to see the Truth, as it is.

Nothing so cripples the spiritual life as these hidden "bugs" in the motor of our soul. They may be any one of several common faults such as self-seeking, bitterness towards others, jealousy and hate. Those who are trying to grow closer to God without self-analysis wonder why they suffer such frequent defeats: invariably it is because of the Trojan Horse within them, the unrecognized dominant fault. Until that is dug out and admitted before God, with a desire to destroy it, there will be no real spiritual progress. As St. Augustine has said, *"He is Thy best servant who looks not so much to hear that from Thee that he himself willeth; as rather to will that which he heareth from Thee."*

CHAPTER 58

Revolution Starts with Man

There are any number of social and economic theories under discussion today, but all plans for changing the world boil down to two: we may reform institutions, or we may reform man.

Most of the blue-print-for-perfection writers begin with the assumption that all the ills of humanity can be charged against an institution, a *thing*: change that, they tell us, and all will be well. Some of their programs blame private property for our troubles, and would "reform" it into collective ownership. Others blame our parliamentary systems, and offer to "reform" them into dictatorships. Others blame the gold policy, and tell us to "reform" it into a silver policy. But in every instance the revolution is to be waged against something *outside* of man; the blame is placed, and the solution sought, in property, or government, or finance. Present-day reformers never blame man himself for the world's debacle, nor try to reform the individual.

This emphasis on institutions as the cure-alls of the world has become so great that many reformers draw up a plan for peace and prosperity . . . and then demand that man himself shall change his nature to fit their plan. Human personality has become insignificant to them; the State is no longer seen as existing for man, but man is told he gains his meaning only in the service he can give the State. Man, under such a system, is de-humanized, de-personalized, poured into a dictatorial pattern, so that he will be molded into a mere servant of a nation, a race or a class.

This stubborn worship of a theory has had most appalling consequences in our day. To the theorist, it does not seem to matter that whole nations are deprived of liberty, that millions starve, that thousands are purged . . . so long as the theory is maintained in power. Instead of making the hat of governmental policy fit the head of man, the modern tendency is to cut off the head if it does not fit the hat . . . to demand that institutions, political schemes and social theories must prevail, no matter if their cost proves to be the destruction of man himself.

But there is a second method of reforming the world. This method is based on the belief that reform must begin with man. It holds that his nature must, indeed, adapt itself . . . but to a larger plan than any temporal theory, than any government or institution or blue-print for world order. This second method agrees that there must be a revolution . . . but not a revolution against something *outside* of man. It urges a revolt against the evil *within* man; his pride, his egotism, his selfishness, his envy and his avarice.

The second kind of revolutionary reform does not place the blame for our troubles on institutions but on humanity . . . not on how man handles his property, but on how man handles himself. This is a less popular method of reform than the first: we all prefer to blame something other than ourselves for our difficulties. The child kicks the door on which he bumped his head; the golfer breaks his club because he did not make the hole. Yet it was the golfer's fault he missed . . . not that of the club, nor of the God Whom he may curse, in his irritation. The world is like the golfer: man forever throws the blame for his troubles away from the one place where it belongs—himself.

Projecting the blame for our difficulties brings no solution, and it never will. For the trouble with the world lies in man. There is no point in transferring the title to property from a few capitalists to a few commissars, if you leave both groups greedy and dishonest. There is no point in tinkering with the rules of parliamentary institutions, when the trouble lies, not in the rules, but in the selfishness of the men who administer them. If we would remake the world, we must begin by remaking the individual man; then the institutions will be good enough, for they will resemble the good men who made them.

And that is why institutions and plans must be supple and elastic enough to fit the free, aspiring spirit of the men who grow and enlarge their vision as they reach toward God. No lesser goal than God Himself is great enough to demand of any man that he transform his nature . . . no human institution has the right to cramp his powers. Man is the highest creature on earth: he matters more than every theory, every government, every plan, for the world and all that it contains are not worth one immortal soul. Let institutions crumble, blueprints go up in smoke, and governments decay. These are mere trivia, compared to the vast question asked of all of us: "How is a man the better for it, if he gains the whole world at the cost of losing his own soul?"

There Is Hope

Our world is full of prophets of gloom, and I would be one of them if I did not practically believe in God. Thirty years ago the one word on everyone's lips was "progress." Now everyone speaks of *defeat* and the *atomic bomb*. This attitude of pessimism varies in direct ratio and proportion to the frequency with which one follows world news. This is not necessarily because world news is depressing, but because one seldom allows time for counterbalancing war news with other factors. As a result people lead *political* lives, not spiritual lives.

It would be interesting to see a commentator take the medical reports of sick patients in hospitals and broadcast them; or to read the headlines after one detail of the report was selected to the exclusion of others. We might read something like this: "Appendix lost! Life despaired!" Tremendous disproportions are created by headlines and news reports, as too often the startling is identified with the true. Parents who live in love and affection for one another, and rear their children for the triple piety of God, neighbor, and country make no headlines. But let Glamorous Glamor separate from her husband after eighteen months of biological unity, and it becomes news. The worst is taken; the good forgotten.

So it is with the war and the world situation. Times are bad! They have never been worse; for never before has a world civilization turned against the Divine Light. We are indeed witnessing the transfer of the Christian heritage from the West to the East. Not that the West will lose it, but that the East will begin to do with it what the West did with it in its Springtime. But despite these facts, this is not the end of civilization; nor are we to be without hope. We have simply reached a moment in history where God is permitting us to feel our inadequacy, so long as we trust only in ourselves. Very often a father will allow his son, who "thinks he knows all about it," to fumble and to err in building his playhouse, until in humility he calls upon the father to help him.

Instead of this being a time of disaster, it is rather a period of humiliation. We are being left to ourselves, to our own devices, to our own conceits. Day by day we are learning that Scriptural truth: "Woe to them that go down to Egypt for help, trusting in horsemen because they are many and in horses because they are strong, and have forgotten the loving God."

A farmer went with his son into a wheatfield to see if it was ready for the harvest. The son pointed to the stems that held up their heads, saying: "Those that let their heads hang cannot be good for much." The father replied: "See here, foolish child. This stalk that stands so straight is lightheaded, and almost good for nothing, while these that hang their heads so modestly are full of beautiful grain." In national life, as in nature, humility, with a head bowed before God, is the beginning of greatness.

Our greatest days are ahead, though in between intervenes the purging, where we will learn that as the rays cannot survive without the sun, so neither can we prosper without God. This hope can be translated into victory in either of two ways: by prayerful rewaking our hearts, or by being brought within an inch of disaster, until from the depths of our insufficiency we cry out to the Goodness of God. The world, and in particular our own country, is filled with thousands and thousands of good people; there is an intensification of spiritual life that is inspiring; intercession has multiplied; the young are craving for spiritual sacrifice. We are not lost! We are only losing our pride. God never puts the crown of victory on a swollen head. As the shadows of the sun are longest when its beams are lowest, so we are greatest when we make ourselves least. Pride slays thanksgiving. Our next greatest victory in making peace will be celebrated by a solemn national act of thanksgiving to God. How far away is it?